THE SCIENCE OF HUMAN POSSIBILITIES

MORE PRAISE FOR *THE SCIENCE OF HUMAN POSSIBILITIES*

"Dr. Murty's book serves as a unique and colorful invitation to lean into a certain hidden wholeness of life, to discover through the integration of ancient teachings and modern science the 'light within.'"

—**Don Morrison,** former Chief Operating Officer of BlackBerry/Research In Motion, Chair of the Board of the Dalai Lama Center for Ethics and Transformative Values at the Massachusetts Institute of Technology (MIT)

"The long philosophical tradition of Vedanta that these reflections are imbued with, from the reading of the classics to the experience of modernity, presents itself as a discipline of individual development, toward the full realization of human possibility."

—**Matilde Marcolli**, Robert F. Christy Professor of Mathematics and Computing and Mathematical Sciences at the California Institute of Technology (Caltech)

"An edifying compendium, brimming with whimsy and peppered with practical advice—such as: keep only a short 'to do' list, or more's the point keep a 'not to do' list. I'm glad to have put reading *The Science of Human Possibilities* on my list of things to do.

—**Siobhan Roberts**, author of *Genius at Play, The Curious Mind of John Horton Conway*

THE SCIENCE OF HUMAN POSSIBILITIES

VIJAYA KUMAR MURTY

Sutherland House Experts

TORONTO, 2024

Sutherland House Experts Corporation
260 Heath Street West
Suite 605
Toronto, Ontario
M5P 3L6

First edition, July 2024

Manufactured in Turkey
Cover designed by Jordan Lunn
Book composed by Karl Hunt

Library and Archives Canada Cataloguing in Publication
Title: The science of human possibilities / V. Kumar Murty.
Names: Murty, Vijaya Kumar, 1956- author.
Description: Includes bibliographical references and index.
Identifiers: Canadiana (print) 20240358945 | Canadiana (ebook) 20240359003 |
ISBN 9781738396405 (hardcover) | ISBN 9781738396412 (EPUB)
Subjects: LCSH: Self-actualization (Psychology) | LCSH: Mind and body. |
LCSH: Ability. | LCSH: Vedanta.
Classification: LCC BF637.S4 M89 2024 | DDC 158.1—dc23

ISBN 978-1-7383964-0-5
eBook 978-1-7383964-1-2

CONTENTS

"You know but little of that which is within you."

—Swami Vivekananda

"The difference between what we do and what we are capable of doing would suffice to solve most of the world's problems."

—Mahatma Gandhi

DEDICATION

To my teachers, who showed me the science of human possibilities.

ACKNOWLEDGMENTS

I have greatly benefited from conversations over the years with many teachers who not only explained their profound ideas but also demonstrated them in practice. I feel an immense sense of gratitude to all of them.

I am also grateful to many monks of the Ramakrishna Order for their invitation to speak at different venues, as these occasions provided an opportunity to explore and deepen my understanding. The essays in this book are largely based on those lectures. In particular, I would like to thank Swami Sarvagatananda and Swami Pramathananda for many invitations to speak in Boston, Providence, and Toronto. In addition, I would like to thank Swamis Kripamayananda, Sarvabhutananda, Sasikantananda, Tyagananda, and Yogatmananda.

I am grateful to Swami Shuddhidananda of the Advaita Ashrama and Managing Editor of *Prabuddha Bharata*, for permission to present expanded and revised versions of the following articles:

Thankfulness and appreciation, *Prabuddha Bharata*, 118 (September, 2013), 535–539

Lead, Kindly Light, *Prabuddha Bharata*, 111 (November, 2006), 584-589, 111 (December, 2006), 654–657

Tradition and innovation in spiritual life, *Prabuddha Bharata*, 116 (August, 2011), 542–548.

I am grateful to Swami Divyakripananda, Editor of *Vedanta Kesari*, for permission to present expanded and revised versions of the following articles:

Dealing with uncertainty, *Vedanta Kesari*, 100(2013), 275–278, 311–316.

Do young people need discipline, *Vedanta Kesari*, 92(2005), 494–497.

I am grateful to Swami Suparnananda, Secretary of the Ramakrishna Mission Institute of Culture, for permission to present an expanded and revised version of the article "The science of human possibilities" from the volume *Total Human Development in the light of Ramakrishna-Vivekananda Tradition*, pp. 80–100, ed. Swami Sarvabhutananda, published by the Ramakrishna Mission Institute of Culture in 2009.

In addition, I am grateful to a number of friends who read through parts of the manuscript at various stages of development, and offered valuable comments and suggestions. In particular, I would like to thank Rina Chakravarti, Eve Goodmon, Deirdre Haskell, Ram Murty, Siobhan Roberts, Neil Seeman, Vijay Shankar, and Meena Singh for their helpful inputs.

Finally, I would like to express my gratitude to Neil Seeman and Sydney Druckman of Sutherland House Experts. Their patience, understanding and encouragement made the entire production process a very positive and pleasant experience!

INTRODUCTION

EVERYONE IS TALENTED. We have only to discover where our talent lies. This perspective has crystallized after more than 40 years of experience in front of the classroom as a professor of mathematics—and as a practicing mathematician collaborating with a global network of peers—in my role as Director of the Fields Institute for Research in Mathematical Sciences. The Institute is a space that brings mathematical scientists together to share ideas and to work together on new discoveries. I see researchers who are early in their career, as well as established mathematicians who are legends in the field. The unscripted, serendipitous interaction and creative efforts of all our visitors are what make the Institute a magical place. I have clearly understood that no one has a monopoly on discovery or talent.

Over the last four decades, I estimate that I have spent at least 17,000 hours instructing small and large classes of university students in mathematics. The students have ranged from novice undergraduates, to those who were completing their PhD thesis. The topics discussed ranged from basic calculus, to making progress on problems that would push forward the frontiers of our knowledge. And I have yet to find a student who I felt was not talented! The structure of our time-constrained, curriculum-confined, results-oriented interaction (especially in introductory classes) might have prevented me from discovering what that particular talent was, but I don't recall any situation where I was not convinced the talent was there. And, thus, my advice to students has always been to discover the talent that lies hidden within them. This is the starting point for what I call "the science of human possibilities."

I had always been passionate about mathematics, both the doing and the communicating of it. It started from a young age, with a recognition that I had some ability in math, but over the years, that matured into the awareness that the doing of mathematics was a very beautiful and highly creative activity. And I think many students have felt that passion and enthusiasm, and were able to benefit from it, even when they were feeling challenged by the actual mathematics. That feeling has led to conversations about attitudes and aspirations, and about beauty and creativity. While it was possible to feel intimidated by the math, beauty and creativity were timeless topics that everyone embraced. It was just a small step from there to begin a conversation on talent and how to uncover it. And I have always found such conversations to be rewarding for everyone involved.

While these ideas were always within me, recognizing their presence, developing them, and articulating them has been an intriguing journey. It began with a summer day in 1978, when my brother Ram and I were perusing the shelves of philosophy books in the MacOdrum library at Carleton University in Ottawa. We were no strangers to the library since, during our undergraduate studies, we had spent many hours there reading and studying—you might say devouring—myriad books and journals. But that was entirely on the floor for Science, and almost entirely in the areas allocated to Mathematics. What was unusual that day was that we were wandering the aisles on the floor for the Humanities.

The week before, we had attended a series of lectures on the *Kena Upanishad*, a short but powerful ancient text in Sanskrit, focusing on the question of the power, or the intelligence, that makes all phenomena possible. *What makes it possible for the eyes to see and the nose to breathe, for the plants to grow, and the planets to orbit?* The Sanskrit word *kena* means 'by whom,' but depending on the context, it could also mean 'how,' 'why,' or 'by what.' The probing question that the *Upanishad* begins with is '*by whose will does the mind think?*' I know that Ram and I were stirred to awe and fascination by the question, and so we listened with rapt attention to the exposition of the *Upanishad*.

I recall that Ram and I had heard about the *Upanishads* as children and knew they were considered very important and very sacred. We mused about what these mysterious works might contain, and why they were held in such high regard. We wondered who would be able to explain these things to us. But every question, and the desire to know its answer, has its gestation period, and it wasn't until both of us were in graduate school (Ram at MIT and I at Harvard) that we got the opportunity to begin exploring the *Upanishads*. And oddly, it was not in Boston, but back in Ottawa where we had grown up, that the opportunity presented itself. It was as if the universe was telling us that the answers were always there in front of us, but that we were not ready for them until now.

The *Kena Upanishad* is one of a number of *Upanishads*, a dense body of largely aphoristic works forming the core of Indian spiritual and philosophical thought. Because of the aphoristic and relaxed style, and the depth of ideas that are presented in these works, large and extensive commentaries have been written on them to explain and organize the intricate thought submerged in the *Upanishads*. Among the many commentators, there are two who stand out in my mind.

The first is that of the ninth-century philosopher and teacher Adi Sankaracharya—commonly referred to as Sankara. He appeared on the scene during the decline of Buddhism in India, and I think one of his greatest contributions was the series of written works in which he systematized the thought and the presentation of the *Upanishads*. Following in the tradition of Gaudapada (his teacher's teacher), Sankara not only presented the spiritual thought but also embedded the free-flowing ideas of the *Upanishads* into a philosophical system. There are scholars who have devoted, and are currently devoting, their entire intellectual life to studying and further elaborating on Sankara's works. This has produced a very rich tradition of scholarship built upon Sankara's perspective.

Both the *Upanishads* and Sankara's works are in Sanskrit, and so if one really wants to understand the thought, one has to master this language, which is both ancient and modern at the same time. Unfortunately, I had not more than a small smattering of knowledge in Sanskrit, and certainly not enough to be able to navigate the works of Sankara. This brings me to the second of the commentators on the *Upanishads* who stand out in my mind. This is the nineteenth-century philosopher and teacher Swami Vivekananda. He burst upon the world scene in 1893 at the Columbian Exhibition in Chicago. This exhibition was to celebrate what at that time was regarded as the 400th anniversary of Christopher Columbus discovering America.[1] By a fortuitous sequence of circumstances, the unknown monk, Vivekananda, stood up to speak at one of the events of the exhibition and made such an impact that he was unknown no more. Thousands would soon come to listen to Vivekananda as he lectured on the philosophy of the *Upanishads* and their practical consequences for navigating ourselves through life in a way that we each can discover fulfillment.

Many important philosophers have noted that we must be discerning in deciding which thinkers merit our time. As Seneca wisely noted, "We must be judicious in selecting the minds we allow to influence us, for our time on this earth is limited."[2] This sentiment was echoed by other notable Stoic philosophers such as Epictetus and Marcus Aurelius, who underscored the importance

1 Christopher Columbus is credited with discovering the Americas in 1492. However, it is important to note that this traditional view has been challenged, as there were indigenous peoples in the Americas long before Columbus's arrival. Additionally, evidence suggests that other non-indigenous groups, such as the Vikings, may have reached the Americas before Columbus. Therefore, while Columbus's voyages were significant in connecting the Americas with the rest of the world, the concept of "discovering" America is complex and has been reevaluated in light of historical and archaeological evidence.

2 See: Seneca's "Moral Letters to Lucilius," also known as the "*Epistulae Morales ad Lucilium.*"

of focusing on wisdom that enriches our lives and aligns with our values amid the constraints of our finite existence. From my point of view, there are many advantages in studying Vivekananda over other thinkers. The first is that (for me) there was no linguistic barrier. Almost all of his works are in English, and so, no translation is required. Moreover, his style of expression is powerful. This is perhaps why one of his contemporaries, American philosopher William James, said of him: "That man is simply a wonder for oratorical power."[3] One of Vivekananda's biographers, the 1915 Nobel Laureate in Literature, Romain Rolland, writes, "His words are great music, phrases in the style of Beethoven, stirring rhythms like the march of Handel choruses. I cannot touch these sayings of his, scattered as they are through the pages of books at thirty years' distance, without receiving a thrill through my body like an electric shock. And what shocks, what transports must have been produced when in burning words they issued from the lips of the hero!"[4]

The second is that Vivekananda's lectures, compared to those of Sankara, are closer to our time period and the style of expression is consequently easier to follow. Moreover, given that many of Vivekananda's most important lectures were delivered outside of India, they are expressed in a way that is less dependent on a

3 The statement occurs in a letter written by James to Mrs. Ole Bull on August 2, 1900, and quoted in Marie Louise Burke, *Swami Vivekananda in the West: New Discoveries*, Volume 4, p. 554, Advaita Ashrama, Mayavati, 1986.

4 R. Rolland, *The Life of Vivekananda and the Universal Gospel*, tr. E. F. Malcolm-Smith, p. 170, Advaita Ashrama, Mayavati, 1931.

cultural familiarity with India. The third advantage in studying Vivekananda over other thinkers is that in his presentations, Vivekananda adopted a scientific perspective, and given that my background was in science (specifically, in mathematics), this resonated well with me.

The fourth advantage is perhaps the most significant. It is that Vivekananda's message was about translating the highest ideals into action. His was a philosophy of how to live life and how to channel your talent to its greatest possible effect. The highest and deepest thought, he said, would have to reflect itself, and be translated into *action*. There was not a separate contemplative life, and an active life, but one life throughout. If the thought pointed to the glory of the human spirit, then action would have to demonstrate the glory of human achievement. As our spiritual nature is latent and currently unknown to us, so is our achievement latent and currently unknown to us. Once again, we are led to 'the science of human possibilities.' Vivekananda buttressed his arguments with the same Upanishadic foundation that Sankara had used to argue for a division between the lives of knowledge and action.

Both Sankara and Vivekananda established monastic traditions to develop and teach their thought. In the case of Vivekananda, this resulted in the Ramakrishna Order of monks, named after Vivekananda's spiritual teacher, Sri Ramakrishna. And the mention of the Ramakrishna Order brings me back to the MacOdrum library at Carleton University in Ottawa where Ram and I were looking for books on the Upanishads. We came across a book called *The Message of the Upanishads*. The author was Swami Ranganathananda, a monk of the Ramakrishna Order.

The book was a collection of transcribed lectures, and, flipping through its pages, I encountered a wonderful expression: 'the science of human possibilities.' This immediately resonated with me and expressed what I had intuitively felt for a long time, namely, the latent potential of every human being. And over several decades, I have had a chance to see this potential play out in the classroom. Every student was talented. The best thing I could do for them was to help them discover their talent. I was in sympathy with the lectures in this book and learnt that a lot of Indian philosophy, especially as it was interpreted and explained by Vivekananda, was concerned with exactly this question of our individual talents and their manifestation.

In the mysterious manner that the Universe works, the following year, Swami Ranganathananda visited Boston. Ram and I were able to meet him in person and listen to him speak. His disciplined posture, his diction, his composure and the extemporaneous fluency of his speech convinced us that 'the science of human possibilities' was a concept that he was living, not just espousing. This was confirmed when we read about his life and discovered that he had had very little formal education and yet was able to share the stage and engage in riveting conversation with leading intellectuals, such as Harvard economist John Kenneth Galbraith and English philosopher and evolutionary biologist Julian Huxley.

Over the intervening decades, I have reflected further on this 'science of human possibilities.' The collection of ideas presented in this book is based on lectures I have given over the years in various contexts on topics connected to 'the science of human possibilities.' The audience for those lectures largely consisted of people familiar with the thought of Vivekananda and of the *Upanishads*. However, I feel that the thought can be of interest to a wider audience, a global audience, and so I have gone through the texts and revised them to make them more suitable for a general audience in the form of this book.

The first chapter is based on a talk given at a memorial conference in honor of Swami Ranganathananda, who passed away in 2005 at the age of 96. I spoke about 'the science of human possibilities' and added to it the perspectives gained from recent developments in neuroplasticity, that is, the brain's proven ability to change and adapt in response to experience, learning, and even injury.

The second and third chapters are about how we can help each other in our journey of discovery of our innate talents and their promise for the world. We can help others through imparting good wishes, and we can benefit from the good wishes of others by keeping our mind in a state of receptivity and gratitude as expressed in a simple 'thank you.'

The fourth chapter is about the method of study as a way of mining our own mind to discover the riches and talents within us.

The fifth chapter addresses the question of doubt and uncertainty that may assail us as we travel on this path of self-discovery of the greatness that lies within.

The sixth chapter discusses the need for discipline as a key transformative tool in manifesting our potential. It is specifically addressed to young people, who, in their eagerness to chart a fresh course for themselves unfettered by the dogma of the past, might fail to recognize the importance of discipline. I take care in the definition of this word, discipline, as it can take on different meanings.

The last three chapters specifically discuss aspects of spiritual life. There is a good deal of confusion on the meaning of spirituality, and, in these essays, I try to throw some light on this subject, especially in the context of illuminating the science of human possibilities. In the seventh chapter, we discuss the relationship between culture and spirituality, and the idea that it is possible to be rooted in one cultural or spiritual tradition, while being open to the wisdom of other traditions. The dynamics of cultural interaction have been studied by many social scientists and there are different points of view on how best to accomplish this. I also discuss the concept of identity which is closely connected to culture.

In the eighth chapter, we discuss a metaphor that occurs in many spiritual traditions, namely that of light. Revealingly, it is a metaphor that recurs in many aspects of human life, both in the sphere of the secular and the sacred. We speak of someone as being 'bright' to indicate that they are intelligent. The chapter discusses a multitude of ways in which we think of light, and, ultimately, converges on our relationship to light. Vivekananda gives the metaphor: "We are lamps, and our burning is what we call life."[5]

In the final essay of this collection, we ask whether innovation has a place in spiritual life. In some traditions, it would be considered blasphemous to speak of anything other than established dogma. Some other traditions are relatively open to new ways of approaching spiritual life. We discuss the relationship between

5 *Complete Works of Swami Vivekananda*, 15th edition, Advaita Ashrama, Mayavati, 1977, Volume 7, p. 38.

tradition and innovation in this context, and the need for both aspects in a spiritual life. They can coexist because they refer to different dimensions of spiritual life. In the context of the science of human possibilities, it is possible to accept some fundamental principles as tradition, while innovating upon the practices by which one apprehends the truth of those principles.

The essays in this collection are an invitation to reflect, and to ascertain how this science can give us a richer experience of our own journey of self-examination and self-actualization in harmony with the world. I have been learning about, and learning from, this science for many years. That learning process is still ongoing as I continue to discover new dimensions of the human being. I invite you to join me on this fascinating journey!

1

THE SCIENCE OF HUMAN POSSIBILITIES

THE SCIENCE OF human possibilities is about identifying, developing, and manifesting the perfection and divinity that is within any human being. Swami Ranganathananda spoke often about this subject. In reviewing his life, one sees that he himself was an exemplar of that science. From humble beginnings and with great effort, he raised himself to become an eloquent expositor, interpreter, and exemplar of the Vedanta philosophy and the thought of Swami Vivekananda.

In November 1859, when Sri Ramakrishna was 23 and 4 years before Swami Vivekananda was born, Charles Darwin published his treatise, *On the Origin of Species by Means of Natural Selection, or the Preservation of Favored Races in the Struggle for Life.* Commonly known as *On the Origin of Species*, Darwin's work documented many species and tried to classify them into families according to levels of organization. The book was controversial as its main thesis was that species did not appear all at once, but evolved. Over a period of time, one species would morph into another species by a natural process. Darwin hypothesized that the main catalyst of this evolutionary process was natural selection and survival. All of his data were taken from the animal and plant kingdoms and his conclusions referred to those domains. However, it was natural to ask whether such processes could apply to humans. While acknowledging that the process probably did apply to humans, Darwin was careful to add that at the human level, mechanisms other than competition and survival play significant roles in evolution.

Darwin's theory was controversial on two fronts. Firstly, it stood against a dominant theological view that species were created by God to populate the earth. Those who held this view felt that the appearance of a multitude of species is a divine process and not a natural one. Secondly, at the other extreme, it spawned a school of thought that attempted to reduce everything in human experience to natural processes at the material level. This school felt that the human being could be understood through purely material processes. Darwin was apprehensive about applying his theories unthinkingly to the human realm, and, on this point, his contemporary, biologist and anthropologist Thomas Huxley rang an alarm: "systematic materialism may . . . destroy the beauty of life."[6]

6 Thomas Huxley, *Methods and Results*, Volume 1, pp. 164-165, Appleton Century Crofts, New York, 1903.

It is, in fact, more than an aesthetic problem. Indeed, evolution at the human level seems to involve new dimensions. In a retrospective on evolution, a century after Darwin, the evolutionary biologist and humanist Sir Julian Sorell Huxley (grandson of Thomas Huxley) wrote: "Man's evolution is not biological but psycho-social; it operates by the mechanisms of cultural tradition . . . Accordingly, major steps in the human phase of evolution are achieved by . . . ideological instead of physiological or biological organization."[7]

He added: "In the light of our present knowledge, man's most comprehensive aim is seen not as mere survival, not as numerical increase, not as increased complexity or organization or increased control over his environment, but as greater fulfillment – the fuller realization of more possibilities by the human species collectively and more of its component members individually. . . . Once greater fulfillment is recognized as man's ultimate or dominant aim, we shall need a science of human possibilities to help guide the long course of psycho-social evolution that lies ahead."[8]

Thus, the arena of evolution at the human level was seen by these thinkers as the realm of the mind and the realm of social interaction. The driving force behind this evolutionary process is the pursuit of fulfillment, at both the individual and collective levels.

This helps us focus on what we might mean by a 'science of human possibilities.' The human being is seen as a repository of infinite

7 Julian Huxley, *Evolution after Darwin*, Volume 3, pp. 251-252, University of Chicago Press, Chicago, 1960.
8 Ibid., pp. 20-21.

possibilities, waiting to be realized. Human potential is infinite, and manifesting talent and ability is what Swami Vivekananda felt to be the essence of education. He insisted that infinite possibilities reside within every individual, and he would not tolerate anyone thinking otherwise.

Swami Vivekananda said: "Do you know how much energy, how many powers, how many forces, are still lurking behind that frame of yours? What scientist has known all that is in man? Millions of years have passed since man first came here, and yet but one infinitesimal part of his powers has been manifested. Therefore, you must not say that you are weak. How do you know what possibilities lie behind that degradation on the surface? You know but little of that which is within you. For behind you is the ocean of infinite power and blessedness."[9]

Moreover, by developing these possibilities, one develops confidence in oneself, and Swami Vivekananda felt this faith in oneself to be the essence of religion. He said: "He is an atheist who does not believe in himself. The old religions said that he was an atheist who did not believe in God. The new religion says that he is an atheist who does not believe in himself."[10]

9 *Complete Works of Swami Vivekananda* (hereafter, referred to as *Complete Works*), Volume 2, p. 299.
10 *Complete Works*, Volume 2, p. 299.

EDUCATION AND EVOLUTION TO PROBE HUMAN POSSIBILITY

Swami Vivekananda was a strong advocate for education as a means for one to identify and develop one's talents, and, in the process, acquire faith in oneself. As we said above, Swami Vivekananda defined education as the manifestation of the perfection already in man. He defined religion as the manifestation of the divinity already in man.[11] He said that there is no limit to the extent that one could evolve in either of these aspects in a single lifetime. The only limit is the one we set ourselves.

To a large extent, this limit is based on our concept of ourselves. There is a beautiful story told by Sri Ramakrishna that illustrates this.[12] Once, a female tiger was stalking a flock of goats. A hunter saw the tiger from a distance and killed her. While dying, she gave birth to a baby tiger. This tiger was taken into the flock by the goats and raised by them. The baby tiger learnt to eat grass and bleat like a goat.

Over the course of time, the tiger grew up. Obviously, it did not become a goat but an adult tiger. Still, it continued to graze on grass and bleat. Another tiger once skulked near the flock, stealthily stalking its prey. It was shocked to see among the flock an adult tiger grazing just like the other goats. It tried to approach the tiger

11 *Complete Works*, Volume 4, p. 358.

12 *Gospel of Sri Ramakrishna*, tr. Swami Nikhilananda, p. 359, seventh printing, Ramakrishna-Vivekananda Center, New York, 1984.

to ask it what it was doing there, but the entire flock, including the grass-eating tiger, fled at the approach of the new tiger. Mystified, the new tiger withdrew and observed the flock for some length of time. Finding an opportunity where the grass-eating tiger was alone, the wild tiger pounced on it and dragged it away to the forest. All the time, the grass-eating tiger was bleating pitifully.

In the forest, the wild tiger let it go and told it forcefully, 'you are a tiger, not a goat.' The grass-eating tiger said, 'No, no, I am a goat. Please don't eat me. Let me go.' At this, the wild tiger dragged it to a pond and said, 'Look at your reflection and look at mine. I am a tiger and so are you.' For the first time, the grass-eating tiger began to doubt that it was a goat. Then the wild tiger gave it some meat and said, 'This is your food, not grass.' The grass-eating tiger started to relish the meat. Finally, the wild tiger said, 'Now roar like a tiger.' The grass-eating tiger now felt more confident and made the attempt at a roar, and was surprised at the sound. Finally, it dawned on the grass-eating tiger that it was in fact a tiger and not a goat, and that it had been a tiger all along.

Sri Ramakrishna said that he heard this story from Tota Puri (one of his teachers), and it is a very apt illustration. Unbeknownst to us, we can be trained to limit ourselves and prevent ourselves from realizing our destiny and manifesting our potential. The science of human possibilities has to deal with this problem and show us a way to solve it.

The solution is good education. It is not just education, but *good* education that is required. Swami Vivekananda explains the difference between education and *good* education: "Education is not the amount of information that is put into your brain and runs riot there, undigested, all your life. We must have life-building, man-making, character-making assimilation of ideas. If you have assimilated five ideas and made them your life and character, you have more education than any man who has got by heart a whole library."[13]

The role of education is to help us to discover both our potential and our limitations. We all have certain abilities and skills. These are more or less developed, according to the interest and attention that we devote to them. If we are interested in something and pay attention to it, that ability will flourish and grow. If we neglect ability, it will slowly wilt like an untended plant. One role of education is to help us to identify our abilities and skills and to help us to nurture them.

Education should also help us to identify our limitations so that we can work to overcome them. We cannot achieve growth by disregarding our limitations. It is crucial to address and manage them systematically and logically, all the while maintaining the confidence that they are surmountable. This self-confidence is what is referred to as *shraddha*. The *Bhagavad Gita* says that one who has this *shraddha* will gain wisdom.[14]

Swami Ranganathananda would often give the example of Nachiketa, the young hero of the *Katha Upanishad* as one who embodied this *shraddha*. Nachiketa was gripped with the question of whether anything survives death. He thought to himself,

13 *Complete Works*, Volume 3, p. 302.
14 *Bhagavad Gita*, '*shraddhavan labhate jnanam*,' Chapter 4, Verse 39.

'Amongst many, I am the best; amongst others, I may be in the middle,'[15] but I am never the last. I can find the solution to this problem. That optimistic attitude toward a problem is what Swami Ranganathananda held up as an ideal for all people, whatever their station in life and whatever their circumstances. A good education arouses that kind of self-confidence. Swami Vivekananda says: "Through education comes faith in one's own self, and through faith in one's own self the inherent Brahman is waking up."[16]

There is no human being alive who does not possess latent abilities and skills. The problem, however, is that we are not allowed to, or we do not allow ourselves, to discover what our abilities and skills are. In an attempt to help us in this process, society puts forward certain abilities and skills that it values. The educational system puts forward certain abilities and skills that it values. These are meant to be helpful suggestions, but more often than not, we take them as prescriptions. The great people in this history of the world were those who were able to break free from these prescriptions, or who were able to modify and tailor those prescriptions to their own personality. The important thing is to discover our abilities and skills for ourselves and not to try and fit into a mold that society has cast for us.

15 *Katha Upanishad*, '*bahunam emi prathamah, bahunam emi madhyamah*,' Chapter 1, Section 1, Verse 5.

16 *Complete Works*, Volume 4, p. 483. The word *brahman* refers to ultimate reality and comes from the Sanskrit root, *brih*, which means vast or expansive. Swami Vivekananda's use of this word here indicates that discovering and manifesting one's abilities is a stepping stone to discovering something fundamentally deeper and vaster about who we are.

One may argue that social cohesion demands that we encourage certain skills and that certain other skills should be discouraged. For example, if someone boasts of an ability to be a pickpocket, should that not be discouraged? Of course, such socially disruptive 'talents' should be discouraged. There is a beautiful teaching of Sri Ramakrishna that explains this. "When a tree is young, it should be fenced all around; otherwise it may be destroyed by cattle."[17] When it grows strong, the fencing can be removed. When a young mind is in its formative and impressionable stage, certainly social values and expectations have to be taught. Certain prohibitions have to be put in place. These comprise the fencing. However, one should understand the temporary nature of this fencing. Once a degree of maturity has been attained, the fencing is not a help but a hindrance.

This does not mean that prohibitions are no longer necessary and that one can do as one pleases. None of us will argue that it is only young people whom we should discourage from engaging in thievery, and that we should let adults do as they please. We cannot exempt anyone from the prohibition against thievery. It means that a maturity has been attained by which external prohibitions are not necessary. We regulate ourselves for our own good and for the good of our community, our society and for the world.

Some may regard the idea of regulating ourselves as a fairy tale, but I don't think it is. By and large, people are law-abiding not just because of the fear of punishment, but because of a sense of right and wrong. I am not saying that it is easy or automatic, but

17 *Gospel of Sri Ramakrishna*, p. 81.

it is certainly possible. I heard a beautiful story in this regard from Swami Pramathananda, the monastic head of the Vedanta Society of Toronto until his passing in 2003. In 1959, many years before coming to Toronto, he was appointed the headmaster of a school in Purulia in West Bengal. Today, this school is famous for its high standards, but when Swami Pramathananda took charge, there were problems with rampant cheating in exams. In order to correct this situation, he initiated some very strict disciplinary measures, but also established a rapport with the students and staff borne of genuine concern for their well-being and success. Within three years, he was able to turn things around to the extent that exams could be held without a proctor. The students regulated themselves, and there was no cheating. Teachers from across the state visited Purulia to find out how this miracle had been made possible.[18]

18 In a retrospective article posted on the website of the school (https://rkmv.org/vidyapith/articles/ourvidyapith.asp), Swami Pramathananda wrote, "In 1961, a weeklong Seminar was held at the Vidyapith, and thirty-six Headmasters and Headmistresses participated. Dr. D. M. Sen inaugurated the event, and Dr. D. N. Roy, Principal of David Hare Training College, was the Director. On the last day, the participants paid a visit to the school. The Annual Examinations were going on. To their surprise, they noticed that there were no invigilators in the examination halls/rooms. After visiting the whole building, they came to my room and asked me how it was possible! I told them that the undoubted honesty of the students had made it possible. This was possible only after a hard struggle for the last three years, with the help of the teachers and other staff! In the evening after prayer, in the prayer hall, Dr. D. N. Roy, the Director of the Seminar, said, "My dear boys, we have been watching you in the playground, dining hall, in the art gallery, and everywhere, and noticed your wonderful sense of discipline, good and courteous manners--with spontaneity and not under pressure or suppression. But today we have seen your examination halls/rooms and there were no invigilators! It was almost unbelievable nowadays! We are carrying with us a great hope that you students of this Vidyapith will be able to establish discipline, patriotism, honesty, and sincerity, in every sphere of life in West Bengal! May God bless you!"

Swami Pramathananda told them that it was not a miracle but the result of a lot of hard effort by many people.

The case of stealing or cheating is straightforward. But there are other rules that are enforced in an educational system, such as evaluation through objective means; this includes demonstrating knowledge of certain texts and the ability to pass examinations. This is an example of fencing that one ought to be able to remove when a degree of maturity has been attained. Not removing such fencing will serve to stunt our growth. Learning material to pass an examination is understandable at a certain stage. However, if we never go beyond that manner of acquiring knowledge through rote demonstration, if we are never able to plunge into great literature or great science, not with a view to reproducing it within a time frame, but rather with an intense desire to truly understand its essence, then we will not have grown. It is only those who are able to plunge into an activity in this way who will be the innovators, the discoverers and the leaders propelling and steering the subject forward.

As stated above, education is the manifestation of perfection already inherent in all people. It is a process of nurturing and growing. What do we mean by perfection? From the point of view of abilities and talents, it means that there is no limit. However high we may have soared, we can soar yet higher. We should not circumscribe ourselves, or unnecessarily limit ourselves in terms of our capabilities, and say, 'this much and no more.'

EVOLUTION AND RELIGION

Julian Huxley already contends that fulfillment of the human being, individually and collectively, is the aim of life. While Huxley stops with psycho-social evolution, Vedanta goes further and says that there is a further dimension, namely, spiritual evolution. The perfection referred to above is not to be understood only in terms of abilities and talents, but rests within a much grander spiritual dimension. This dimension is not only a natural fulfillment of psycho-social evolution, but it also strengthens the philosophical basis for the science of human possibilities.

According to Vedanta, the essence of the human being is neither matter nor mind, but spirit. As to what spirit is, we can say that it is not matter and it is not mind. Positively, we can say that it is Being (the Sanskrit word is *sat*). The word Being is used as a noun and not as a verb. As Swami Sarvagatananda explains, the nature of this Being is love and consciousness.[19] The spiritual nature of the individual is what gives philosophical sanction to the science of human possibilities. As an embodiment of Divinity, and of spirit, infinite are the possibilities of the manifestation of Being.

At our present stage, we are not aware of ourselves as Being. Rather, we are aware of ourselves as body and mind. According to Vedanta, becoming aware of Being is the goal of life. All of our efforts in life have that one aim in view, either knowingly or

19 Swami Sarvagatananda, *God Is Everything: Isavasya Upanishad, An exposition*, p. 31, Vedanta Society of Toronto, Toronto, 2001.

unknowingly, namely, the awareness that we are pure spirit. In Swami Vivekananda's words: "Each soul is potentially divine. The goal is to manifest this Divinity within."[20]

Moreover, the struggle to realize that we are pure spirit mainly takes place in the psycho-social milieu. Progress in that struggle is what we term spiritual evolution. Through the practice of various disciplines, one begins to be aware of one's spiritual dimension. However, the concept of evolution is used with a different emphasis in Vedanta. Change is the manifestation of that which is already within. What is within is manifested. Patanjali gives the example of water irrigating a field. The field is lined with ridges so that water flows in a specific path. When the ridge is removed, water flows by itself. Once the obstruction is removed, that which is within manifests itself.

Vedanta applies this principle to knowledge and concludes that all knowledge is within. Vivekananda elaborates: "No knowledge comes from outside; it is all inside. What we say a man 'knows,' should, in strict psychological language, be what he 'discovers' or 'unveils'; what a man 'learns' is really what he 'discovers,' by taking the cover off his own soul, which is a mine of infinite knowledge." He continues, "All knowledge, therefore, secular or spiritual, is in the human mind. In many cases it is not discovered, but remains covered, and when the covering is being slowly taken off, we say, 'We are learning,' and the advance of knowledge is made by the advance of this process of uncovering."[21]

20 *Complete Works*, Volume 1, p. 257.
21 *Complete Works*, Volume 1, p.28.

Applying this principle to becoming aware of one's spiritual dimension, Vedanta asserts that we do not become spirit; we *are* spirit. Only we are not aware of this now, and we become aware of this by removing the obstacles that obscure our awareness. This removal of the obstacles is what Vedanta understands by the concept of evolution.

Whether we accept the Vedantic view of spiritual fulfillment, or whether we limit ourselves to fulfillment in the sense of Julian Huxley's humanism, the arena of the evolutionary process is the mind. Regarding the spiritual struggle, the *Katha Upanishad* says, 'By mind alone is it to be attained.'[22] Sri Ramakrishna says, 'In mind one is bound, in mind one is free.' But even if one were not interested in the question of spiritual evolution, even if we were only interested in existential questions of happiness, quality of life, a sense of accomplishment, fulfillment and belonging, even in this case, the arena of our struggles is centered on the mind. Thus, whether we view this from the point of view of a spiritual aspirant, or from the point of view of accomplishment and fulfillment in life, we have to pay attention to the mind. It is through the mind that we can realize our possibilities. The science of human possibilities is all about shaping the mind to be what we are destined to be, to realize and manifest our full potential.

22 *Katha Upanishad*, '*manasaivedam aptavyam*,' Chapter 2, Section 1, Verse 11.

THE REGENERATIVE ABILITY OF THE BRAIN

The biggest obstacle in this process of manifesting our hidden talents, our latent possibilities, is ourselves. We tend to put a limit on ourselves. It has become a habit to think 'this much, and no more.' The science of human possibilities rejects this view. It does not accept an upper bound on what a human being can achieve. The *Bhagavad Gita* states, 'Lift yourself by yourself. You are your own friend and you are your own enemy.'[23] If one has disciplined one's mind, if one has overcome negative ways of thinking, if one has developed *shraddha*, then one is one's own friend. With such a mind, we will never think that a task at hand is impossible. Neither will we be naïve about its complexity. We will correctly assess the difficulty level and devise the means to resolve it.

Swami Ranganathananda would often quote from advances in physics to illustrate concepts related to mind and spirit. Today, advances in the life sciences are assuming a similar role in terms of the revolutionary concepts that are being introduced. In particular, some recent discoveries in the field of neuroscience provide us with physiological support for the science of human possibilities.

We know that our body is composed of many cells. These cells are born and they die, and they are replaced with new cells. We also know that cells specialize into functions; thus, there is a nerve cell, a skin cell, and so on. A brain cell is called a neuron. Neurons,

23 *Bhagavad Gita*, Chapter 6, Verse 5.

also known as nerve cells, are the fundamental units of the brain and nervous system. They are responsible for sending and receiving electrical and chemical signals, and they transmit information to other neurons, muscles, and tissues throughout the body. Though skin cells, for example, regenerate and replenish themselves, it was once thought that brain cells do not. In other words, whatever neurons one has by the time of maturity is the limit. In a sense, this puts a limit on our ability to think. Moreover, as these neurons age and die, it was felt that they were not replaced. As a result, it was anticipated that cognitive abilities would diminish inevitably with age.

This model seemed to provide a physiological basis for the tendency to feel that in youth, one has many possibilities, but by the time one has reached a mature age, many of these possibilities seem to have been curtailed and many are no longer accessible.

This is now known to be not exactly true. Neurons do in fact replenish themselves. It is possible for a brain to continue to maintain or even increase its supply of neuronal cells. Therefore, the idea that thinking power *must* degenerate with age is false. Owing to the existence of neuronal stem cells in the human brain, which were only discovered in 1998, we are gaining greater clarity into how our brain re-energizes itself.[24]

Stem cells are cells that have the ability to specialize themselves in different ways. A stem cell can become a nerve cell, a skin cell,

24 Eriksson PS, Perfilieva E, Bjork-Eriksson T, Alborn AM, Nordborg C, Peterson DA, Gage FH, Neurogenesis in the adult human hippocampus. *Nat Med.* 1998;4: 1313–1307.

and so on. That stem cells could become neurons was a relatively recent discovery. About 40 years ago, they were discovered in rats, and about 30 years ago, they were discovered in birds. There is considerable ongoing research to understand the mechanisms behind neuronal stem cells in humans. But the critical implication from this body of work is that the brain, like other parts of the body, continues to regenerate itself with fresh cells.[25]

MAINTAINING A HEALTHY BRAIN

Now that we understand the regenerative powers of the brain, then the science of human possibilities is obliged to ask: By what methods can we maintain and fuel the health of our brains, both in terms of ensuring the longevity of existing neurons and in terms of availing ourselves of an abundant supply of new neurons. Ongoing research (which is still in its early stages) seems to suggest two methods that we should be aware of. One is physical exercise and the second is learning.

25 Neuroplasticity, also known as neural plasticity or brain plasticity, is a well-documented process that involves adaptive structural and functional changes to the brain. It is the brain's ability to change its activity in response to intrinsic functions or connections. This phenomenon has been extensively documented in scientific literature. For example, a study published in *Frontiers in Cellular Neuroscience* in 2019 discusses the impact of studying brain plasticity, highlighting the fundamental property of neural plasticity in nervous systems across various species. Additionally, a review published in *Neural Plasticity* in 2014 provides an overview of adult neuroplasticity, emphasizing more than 40 years of research in this field. These sources, among others, contribute to the extensive scientific evidence supporting the concept of neuroplasticity.

Physical exercise seems to trigger the 'anticipatory proliferation'[26] of neuronal stem cells. It is as if the body is anticipating new challenges which will require additional brain power. In general, physical exercise improves the blood supply to the brain, making us feel more alert. It is not necessary to overdo it: one is not trying to become a professional wrestler. Simple cardiovascular exercise such as brisk walking is sufficient. In addition to improving the blood supply to the brain, recent studies suggest that exercise also stimulates a neuronal growth factor. Exercise thereby accelerates our intellectual prowess and sustains our will to seek out and solve ever more challenging problems.

Learning something new seems to enhance the longevity of existing neuronal stem cells. There are studies that show how increased education seems to offer better protection from mental decline and degeneration. It is not the material that is learnt, and certainly not the degree or the diploma conferred, but rather it is the workout that your brain undergoes–from the intellectual analogue of the swishing of jumping ropes, clanging weights, or from steady footsteps up a hillside–which is salient to your intellectual sustenance. The enduring process of learning stimulates the formation of new neuronal pathways and associations.[27]

26 See, for example, van Praag H, Neurogenesis and exercise: past and future directions. *Neuromolecular Med.* 2008;10(2):128–140. doi: 10.1007/s12017-008-8028-z. Epub 2008 Feb 20. PMID: 18286389.

27 In discussions with colleagues, several questions were raised. The first is what we mean by learning. Would memorization stimulate new neuronal pathways as much as a deeper study or understanding? I would say that new neuronal pathways are created according to the perceived need. The brain will respond to the demand that is put on

This confers a new perspective on education, especially for the elderly. Education is not a matter of knowledge acquisition, but of mental health and quality of life. Medicines can keep our body functioning well to some extent, but what keeps our mind functioning well? Health care systems are struggling to address this very important aspect of our life. Without a healthy mind, our quality of life degenerates.

In fact, this principle is relevant to all of us, regardless of our age. We have to pay attention to the health of our mind. If our mind is not well nurtured, we will find it difficult to hold on to what we have, not to speak of attaining new heights.

From this point of view, we may look for activity that exercises our mind. Toward this goal, I offer two concrete suggestions. One is to learn a new language and the other is to learn to draw. Learning a new language improves memory, and it seems to turn on the control system for plasticity of the brain. Language skills develop our verbal and analytic left hemisphere. Learning to draw improves our visual, perceptual right hemisphere.

it, just as the muscles do. If we accept this, then the question is really whether deeper study puts a greater demand on the brain. I suspect that it does as it appeals to not only memory (as memorization does), but also to other faculties such as imagination and intuition. The second question is about the relationship between the brain and mind. This is harder to answer as the scientific community is divided on the issue of whether there is a difference between the brain and the mind. My own view is that they are different.

THE YOGA OF SMALL STEPS

Another issue that the science of human possibilities must deal with is the presumed limitation caused by past experience. 'I was not able to do this in the past, so I will not be able to do it in future.' This kind of thinking is a common experience and mind reflex that discourages us from attempting the tasks that we wish we could do.

This kind of thinking contains the hidden assumption that the abilities of the mind remain static. However, we all know that this is not the case. We go to school and take a course on a subject that we know nothing about. After some lessons, we find that we have acquired some knowledge of the subject. If we apply our mind, then by the end of the course, we would have reached a certain level of proficiency. If on the first day of the course, I was asked a question about the subject, I would not have been able to answer. Would it have been correct for me to surmise that I would *never* be able to answer the question? Certainly not: The course itself guides me and helps me to slowly acquire the ability to answer the question.

One will note, however, that one has to *apply* the mind. To 'apply the mind' means to be interested and to pay attention. These two aspects of the mind at work – interest and attention – are what give thoughts power. These are the tools at our disposal to encourage certain thoughts and to discourage certain other thoughts. If we compare our mind to a garden, interest and attention are the gardener's tools to weed out the bad plants, to aerate the soil and to water it. Sri Ramakrishna used to sing a song:

"Oh mind, you do not know how to farm. Fallow lies the field of your life. If you had only worked it well, how rich a harvest you might reap!"[28]

Also, one will note that the course of instruction takes us step by step from where we are to where we want to be. It is not the case that we attempt everything all at once on the first day. We begin with small steps. If we examine our own life, we may see the things that we would like to do but which seem to remain undone for many years. Perhaps what keeps them undone is that they appear too big and complicated and we are intimidated by that. If we could devise our own 'course' in which we divide up the big task into small steps, then we would have a place to start. It is said that the first step is the hardest. Once that is taken, each successive step becomes simpler. The solution to procrastination, the solution to unfulfilled dreams, the solution to unrealized possibilities, is to start. Begin the task in any way that you can, and think of reaching the goal in terms of the next step to be taken.

This idea of 'the yoga of small steps' applies equally well to our spiritual life. We may ask ourselves why it is that after years of practicing meditation, we don't seem to be any more proficient at it than when we started. The answer is that we have not broken the task up into small steps. We still think that to meditate, we must sit down and at once become absorbed like Buddha. In fact, there are many preparatory small steps that have to be taken first.

28 *Gospel of Sri Ramakrishna*, p. 251.

We speak of meditation, but consider the simpler task of falling asleep. We don't just plant ourselves on a sofa or bed and expect to fall asleep. We make preparations. We wear loose, comfortable clothes. We lie on a bed that is comfortable and not too soft or too hard. We turn the lights out so that we are not distracted by other things. Then we lie down and free our mind from anxieties and cares, and then we wait. Then the magical moment arrives and we fall asleep. We actually don't know how we fell asleep. What we know is all the preparations we went through. We also know when we awake that a certain amount of time has passed and perhaps we feel rested. From this, we surmise that we were asleep. Meditation has to be similarly approached in terms of preparation. The step that we find most difficult, of course, is to free our mind from anxieties and cares. We do this when we go to sleep, and we need to try and do it when we sit for meditation.

NEUROPLASTICITY OF THE BRAIN

The idea that the brain adapts itself to accommodate the efforts to accomplish a task or reach a goal is supported by recent advances in the science of the brain. Beginning with the breakthrough experiments pioneered by the late Wilder Penfield, the McGill neurosurgeon and neurologist, scientific investigators discovered that there seemed to be a correlation between various functions (seeing, hearing, talking, and so on) and activity in specific regions of the brain. Penfield's experiments seemed to suggest that one could draw a 'map' of the brain with each region being allocated a function. Though Penfield did not say so, others after him assumed that these functional maps are static. In other words, they are more or less the same for everyone, and once they are established, they do not change.

Recent work shows that these functional maps are in fact dynamic, and not static. In other words, the maps change. In some sense, we knew this from a folklore perspective. If someone is blind, then what happens to the part of the brain that processes images? Does it simply remain idle? Does the physiological defect of the eye also result in an underutilization of brain space? The answer is "no." That part of the brain is drawn upon to perform other functions. Perhaps sound, smell, or some other sensory processing is performed in that space. In other words, the amount of brain space dedicated to processing sound or smell *increases*. This is why we see that those who are, for example, blind, have a heightened ability in some other sense such as smell or sound. Learning a new skill like playing a musical instrument, studying new philosophical texts, or speaking a new language involves neuroplasticity as the brain adapts, or 'rewires itself,' to these new activities. This dynamic property of brain maps is neuroplasticity and is a subject of intense current study. It is of great interest in the medical community, both in research as well as in clinical practice.[29]

From the point of view of Vedanta, there is no question that neuroplasticity exists. Vedanta clearly says that the material universe

29 N. Doidge, *The Brain that Changes Itself: Stories of Personal Triumph from the Frontiers of Brain Science*, p. 48, Viking, New York, 2007.

is a manifestation of spirit. Desire and intense thought make physical changes possible. They also make physical manifestation possible.

A dramatic example of this is recorded in the life of Sri Ramakrishna. We know that when he meditated intensely on Hanuman,[30] his coccyx (the lower end of the backbone) was slightly extended, as if it were the beginning of a tail. The experience is described in *Sri Ramakrishna, the Great Master* by Sri Ramakrishna himself: "At that time, I had to walk, take my food and do all other actions like Mahavir. I did not do so of my own accord, but the actions so happened of themselves. I tied my cloth round my waist so that it might look like a tail and moved about jumping; I ate nothing but fruits and roots, which again I did not feel inclined to eat when skinned. I spent much of my time on trees and always cried 'Raghuvir, Raghuvir!' with a deep voice. Both my eyes assumed a restless expression like those of the animals of that species, and strange to say, the lower end of the backbone lengthened at that

30 Hanuman is a character in the famous epic *Ramayana*. Also known as Maruti and Mahavir, this character has a lot to teach us about the science of human possibilities. He is a *vanara* or a forest dweller, though in popular description, he is portrayed as a monkey. The *vanara* population befriended Rama and offered to help him find Sita, but they were not disciplined or focused. Hanuman was unusual in that he had both of these traits. He had an unwavering laser-like focus on Rama, and he was very disciplined and even learned. He knew Sanskrit unlike the other *vanaras* and was able to converse directly with Rama. He seems to have been an expert in Raja Yoga as well, if we are to understand how he was able to fly and travel long distances, how he was able to change his size to very large or very small, and how he was able to make himself invisible. However we may understand all of these attributes and abilities, the character of Hanuman is one of the bright lights of the Ramayana as he sets a high standard for devotion, discipline, and determined action.

time by nearly an inch." He continued to metamorphose in this manner such that, as the mood of Hanuman ceased, in the course of time the backbone slowly assumed its previous natural size.[31]

It is said that the cause of rebirth is unfulfilled desires. Those desires propel the *jiva* to seek the materials and means by which they can be fulfilled. This is why it is taught that if one wants to transcend the cycle of birth and death, then one should try to become desireless.

Sufficient desire combined with effort seems to create neuronal associations that affect the functional map of the brain. Neurons communicate with each other by firing an electrical signal. Each neuron is not actually in physical contact with other neurons. Rather, there is a microscopic distance between neurons called the synapse. When a neuron fires near a particular synapse, neurotransmitters are released into the synaptic cleft. These neurotransmitters then bind to receptor molecules on the membrane of the receiving (postsynaptic) neuron, influencing the likelihood of the postsynaptic neuron firing. The neurotransmitters released can either excite or inhibit the postsynaptic neuron, thereby influencing the continuation or inhibition of the signal. From this point of view, one may view the firing of neurons as a physiological manifestation of thoughts. If a sequence of neurons tends to fire together, a habit, a tendency, or a way of thinking is crystallized.

31 Swami Saradananda, *Sri Ramakrishna, The Great Master*, tr. Swami Jagadananda (original in Bengali), Volume 1, pp. 182-183, 5th edition, Sri Ramakrishna Math, Mylapore, 1978.

In this regard, there is a principle known as Hebb's Law: neurons that fire together wire together.[32] In other words, each time neuron B fires after neuron A, the tendency for this sequence to repeat is increased, and, in that sense, they are 'wired together.' The same principle, from a psychoanalytic point of view, may be seen in Sigmund Freud's "law of association by simultaneity." This concept was one of the first scientific understandings put forth by Freud and is linked to his theory of free association. Free association, the psychoanalytic technique developed by Freud, involves exploring the unconscious mind by allowing thoughts to flow freely without censorship or judgment. Enlightenment philosopher John Locke's "law of association," a concept related to his philosophy of mind, expressed a similar concept: simple ideas can become associated in the mind through experience, and this process of association serves as the foundation for the development of more intricate, complex ideas. Locke's theory suggests that our understanding and knowledge are built upon these interconnected associations, allowing us to form a coherent and comprehensive understanding of the world around us based on our experiences and perceptions.

The mind is a complex associating machine. One sensation triggers a flurry of thoughts; these thoughts trigger other thoughts and this cascade continues. Why a particular sensation or thought triggers another particular thought can only be answered empirically as saying that one thought is 'associated' to the other thought. Each

32 N. Doidge, *The Brain that Changes Itself*, p. 63.

thought is associated with many other thoughts and so the flow of thoughts is not quite predictable. On the other hand, there may be dominant patterns in associations that are predictable. If we initiate a thought stimulus, and observe what thought (or more coarsely, what 'species' of thoughts) occurs next, one can uncover the network of associations and thus derive an insight into our individual way of thinking. This is the basis of Freud's psychoanalytic technique of 'free association.'

It is also stated in Vedanta as one of the steps in Raja Yoga, namely, *pratyahara*. In the eight-step path outlined by Patanjali, the first two are about moral and ethical excellence. The next two are about physical well-being. The fifth step, *pratyahara*, is the first psychological step in the entire method and has to do with observation. In this step, one observes thoughts without holding any thought, without identifying with any thought. As a silent witness, one observes the way one thought associates with another. Whereas Freud's method required the intermediacy of the psychiatrist and the translation of thoughts into words, in *pratyahara*, one observes thoughts without translating them into verbal form, gestures, or into any other form of expression. Moreover, in this process, one is both the patient and the doctor.

REALIZING OUR POSSIBILITIES

From this discussion, we see that there is physiological support for the science of human possibilities. Each of us is laden with talents and abilities, and it is up to us to make the effort necessary to manifest them. However, the greatest wonder of human nature is not in what we can aspire to do, but in what we are.

In the first instance, we are human. We distinguish ourselves by our humanity. Swami Ranganathananda spoke of animals reacting to stimuli in a predictable manner. If you approach a cow with straw it will come toward you. On the other hand, if you approach it with a stick it will run away. The animal is chained by its nature. A human being has the possibility of overcoming nature. If someone speaks words of anger or hatred, we need not respond with similar sentiment. We have a choice. We can engage in internal processing to address afflictive emotions such as anger and hatred, and employ positive-energy emotions to provide soothing and healing effects. Negative emotions such as anger and hatred can thereby transform into a form of loving-kindness (*maitrī* in Sanskrit and *mettā* in Pali). Thus, every human being carries this tremendous possibility of choosing how to react, and, in so doing, can reorient his afflictions. This transformation is what we call character.

In the second instance, we are neither matter nor mind; we are spirit. The greatest possibility latent in us is that our spiritual nature can be realized. We can experience that dimension. Not only *can* we do so, but the purpose of human life *is* to do so. Human perfection consists in manifesting, or becoming more fully aware, of our spiritual nature.

In this journey to our spiritual destiny, the arena of effort to improve ourselves is the mind. Therefore, all of the above discussion about unleashing the power of the mind still applies. Through our various efforts to manifest our talents, in transforming our nature and establishing character and in realizing our spiritual nature, we will eventually realize the truth of the statement that our greatest talent is the ability to 'be.'

In turn, this has another important implication. Spirit is unique. The spiritual essence in me is the same as the spiritual essence in you and in everyone else and in all of existence. Upon realizing this, our efforts cannot be restricted to our own well-being, but must extend to the maximization of the well-being of all. Moreover, these efforts at collective well-being are not advanced through help, but rather through worship. It is the worship of God in man.

This was the great ideal that Swami Vivekananda put before all of us. This is why he said, "May I be born again and again and suffer thousands of miseries, so that I may worship the only God that exists, the only God I believe in – the sum total of all souls, and above all, my God the wicked, my God the miserable, my God the poor of all races, of all species, is the special object of my worship."[33] In his famous poem, *To a Friend*, he writes, 'Who loves all beings without distinction, He indeed is worshipping best his God.'[34]

33 *Complete Works*, Volume 5, p. 137.
34 *Complete Works*, Volume 4, p. 496.

2

THE POWER OF GOOD WISHES

INTRODUCTION

THE START OF a new year is an occasion for making resolutions about what we will and will not do during the coming year.[35] It is an attempt to reflect on and express our aspirations and our ideals, as they apply to us and to others. However, it is well known that these resolutions, though formulated and expressed with great sincerity, often lapse. The promise of a new beginning generates a wave of euphoria, on the crest of which rides a newfound sense of purpose. This sense of purpose, in its turn,

35 Adapted from a talk at the Vedanta Society of Toronto on Sunday, January 7, 2007.

spawns a flurry of resolutions and earnest wishes. However, the wave fails to keep its coherence and soon dissolves into nothingness, along with the purpose and the resolutions. The year passes by and after twelve months, we are chagrined to find that no progress has been made on the resolutions. In fact, it may be that we have completely forgotten that we even made such resolutions. Yet, we repeat this exercise year after year. The question naturally arises whether this resolution-setting is all an act of futility.

Amid this phenomenon of lapsed ambition, we habitually offer our good wishes to people in our social or professional milieu. We often say "good luck" or "best wishes," even to casual acquaintances. During the holiday season, we seek and give blessings. We send greeting cards filled with wishes of a happy and bright future. Do these expressions have any power, or are they merely social niceties and linguistic artifacts of our culture?

In this chapter, we shall explore what we mean by good wishes and whether they have any power or not in advancing the science of human possibilities. In a sense, we already know that good wishes do wield certain power. Think of all the great spiritual teachers that the world has known. For some of them, we know their names and something about their lives. For others, we don't know anything about their identity. But their good wishes and blessings, expressed through their thoughts and their everlasting teachings, are sustaining all of us. Centuries and even millennia later, we continue to study their teachings, benefiting from the enduring wisdom they offer. So, clearly good wishes do have some power.

But what if we bring the discussion down to the level of our everyday interpersonal relationships? We may grant that the good wishes of great saints have power even over long periods of time. But what of the wishes that we routinely express to each other? And if we agree that good wishes do have power, then what implications does this observation have for the way we live our lives?

WHAT IS A WISH?

The thesaurus proffers a number of words to help us understand the meaning of the noun *wish*. Among them are desire, aspiration, hope, yearning, longing, craving, fancy, inclination, and want. Certainly, these synonyms give us an idea of the meaning of the word. Note that all of these terms make sense in relation to something that we do not possess at the moment, but which we wish to possess. It could be a material object, a position, or a state of being that is sought after.

A wish can be made for oneself or for someone else. A wish can even be made for some*thing* else. For example, we can wish for the well-being of our country. A national anthem usually contains such a wish. On certain special occasions, we are asked to make a wish. At birthday celebrations, one is told to make a wish, but not to tell anyone what that wish is, for otherwise it might not come true. When one visits a holy place, we bow down in front of the altar and make wishes, praying for certain outcomes.

What, then, is a good wish? It is a wish that leads to some benefit or advantage to whomever it is directed at. We should be aware that a good wish for one person may be, either explicitly or implicitly, a bad wish for someone else. If we wish for the success of one person, we are implicitly wishing for the failure or diminution of someone in competition with that person. Let us ignore for a moment this issue and the moral or ethical question of what constitutes goodness. The question is whether the fact that one expresses such a wish, either for oneself or for another, results in any benefit.

The answer is that it depends on the sender and the recipient. There has to be a fitness to send and a fitness to receive. This applies even if the sender and the recipient are one and the same person. But when both of these are satisfied, then good wishes can definitely yield a good and tangible effect.

ENCOURAGEMENT

Before we delve into details, there is one obvious aspect of good wishes that can and often does have a good effect, and this is encouragement.

We know that in general, encouragement is usually beneficial. If we are struggling to accomplish something, the fact that someone says a few words of encouragement can be very important. This helps us to overcome doubts we may have about our ability to succeed. It helps us to rejuvenate and refresh ourselves if we are tired. The significance is greater if the words come from someone whom we greatly respect and admire.

There are circumstances, however, in which encouragement is not beneficial. Suppose someone is trying to do something that is clearly destructive or damaging. Under such circumstances, encouraging that individual is incitement and would be harmful. In fact, a well-wisher should discourage the individual from that course of action. Before giving encouragement, we should try to ascertain that the individual's efforts are worthy of being encouraged.

Even if the recipient is not struggling to accomplish something, a few words of encouragement can plant a seed in their mind that leads them to start making attempts in a particular direction. Perhaps there was a vague idea implanted in our minds. A good wish from someone whom we revere can elevate that idea from a vague notion to an intense and urgent desire. Sometimes, we are not sure of our priorities. We may have many things that we wish to accomplish. If a person of wisdom and benevolence bestows a blessing upon us that a certain task be finished, that good wish itself will elevate the particular task to a position of utmost importance on our list of priorities.

A famous example of the power of encouragement is the case of Hanuman. A devoted follower and supporter of Sri Rama, Hanuman was often not aware of his own strength and potential. It took Jambuvantha and others in his community to convince him that he had the power to fly to Lanka to find whether Sita was confined there. Their words served to enable Hanuman to tap into the strength that resided within him.

Even the author of the *Ramayana* was not aware of his own potential. In his earlier life, Valmiki had been, in fact, a highway robber. Once, the sage Narada was passing by and Valmiki tried to steal from him. The sage asked him why he was stealing. Valmiki was at first taken aback by the question, but upon reflection, he said he stole to support his family. In that case, Narada asked, would his family members share in the sin he was committing?

Taken aback again by a question that had never occurred to him, he replied that of course they would. Narada asked him to make sure of this, and asked Valmiki to tie him up so that he could not escape while Valmiki went to confirm that his family members would, in fact, share in his sin. Valmiki then strode off to inform his family members that he was a highway robber who engaged in thievery and sometimes even murder to support them; he was stunned to find his family express disgust and assert emphatically that in no way would any part of his sin be shared by them. Rebuked in this way by those whom he loved and who he thought loved him, Valmiki went back to Narada, untied him, told him what happened, and begged for his guidance.

Narada told him that only God gives us unconditional love, and forgives us for our shortcomings and wrong actions. He suggested that Valmiki should repeat the name of God and taught him the *mantra* of Rama, an incarnation of God. Valmiki sat in one place and devoted himself night and day to repeating this *mantra*, so much so that an anthill formed around him. The name, Valmiki, literally means one who is born from an anthill. When Valmiki arose from his meditation, he was indeed born again. He was no longer a highway robber, but a sage.

It is interesting that in *Sanskrit*, the word for sage and poet is the same: *kavih*. This word means 'seer,' and the idea is that both the poet and the sage are able to see beyond the surface. Valmiki was surprised to find that his speech had undergone a change. His was no longer the coarse tongue of a highway robber, but the beautiful language of a poet. He now expressed even ordinary sentiments in a beautiful, poetic form. Valmiki was surprised when he was told by Brahma that he should now write the story of Rama, a narrative that is rich in moral and ethical teachings. Valmiki's work, the *Ramayana*, is revered as a sacred text in Hinduism.

Therefore, encouragement is one way in which good wishes wield power. It plants a seed of potential or of the possible, and causes the listener to act in a manner that will confirm that faith.

However, we know that not all encouragement produces the same effect. Suppose one blesses an individual who has never flown a plane that she might become the best pilot in the air force. Let us further imagine that as a group, we provide significant encouragement to the individual, affirming that she 'can do it.' Will these good wishes and encouragement be fruitful? It may or may not be so. It depends on whether the encouragement and good wishes are in tune with the basic ability, ideals, and temperament of the individual. Good wishes help someone to discover their own abilities and potential. What is within is uncovered and manifested. The effect of good wishes is therefore dependent on the one who wishes, but also on the one who receives the wishes. The *Katha Upanishad* says, "*ascarya vakta, kuṣalasya labdha*" – the speaker must be remarkable and the listener must be qualified.

The speaker must be remarkable in the sense that his words are born of intuition and insight, and not contrived or meant to flatter. The listener must be qualified in the sense that he should have an open mind – one that is ready to listen to suggestion and guidance and to act with determination when in receipt of a wise and benevolent wish.

Related to encouragement is suggestion. Suggestion will be fruitful if it can link to an existing aspiration, possibly dormant or unexpressed, within the recipient. Hypnosis is based on suggestion. Through its power, people are able to overcome bad habits that they were previously unable to shake off.

However, the risk with suggestion lies in its potential to evoke both negative and positive aspirations. For instance, if an individual leans toward excessive ambition, a suggestion that reinforces this trait will be readily embraced. Consider, for example, the Scottish king Macbeth. In Shakespeare's drama, Macbeth was a nobleman but not yet king. On a fateful ride through the country, he chances across three 'witches.' They hail him as 'Thane of Cawdor,' and, finally, as king. Another nobleman who is with him notes his reaction, "Good sir, why do you start?" Macbeth collects himself and is later able to protest 'the Thane of Cawdor lives; why do you dress me in borrowed robes?'[36] Yet, the suggestion planted by the witches finds fertile ground in the ambition lurking in Macbeth's mind. It breeds so aggressively that, in a short time, it completely dominates his mental landscape. A tendency which in the first place should have been restrained has now been exacerbated. How this leads to his ruin is beautifully documented by Shakespeare:

> I have no spur
> To prick the sides of my intent, but only
> Vaulting ambition, which o'erleaps itself
> And falls on th'other. (*Macbeth*, Act 1, Scene 7)

36 W. Shakespeare, "Macbeth," Act 1, Scene iii, in: *William Shakespeare: The Complete Works*, pp. 1046-1047, Gramercy Books, New Jersey, 1975.

Those good wishes are powerful where the wisher is able to see the positive and constructive potential of an individual and, making explicit reference to it, calls it out, or quickens its manifestation. That is why we seek out individuals whom we believe possess insight when we seek blessings. Their well-intentioned blessings serve to nurture our positive aspirations while helping to restrain those ambitions that may not be beneficial for us.

THE TWO COMPONENTS OF A GOOD WISH

In order for a good wish to be fruitful, there are two components in the form of equal participants: the wisher and the wished. The powers within both have to unite. Good wishes act like a spark to ignite a flame within. But there has to be a spark to start with and there has to be something to ignite.

The great ninth-century philosopher and teacher of Vedanta, Sankaracharya, begins many of his works with a preamble in which the qualifications of those who are fit to study the work are enumerated. For example, in his famous analytic work, *Vivekachudamani*, verse 13 states: "Success depends essentially on a qualified aspirant; time, place and other such means are but auxiliaries in this regard." In verse 17, it is noted that '[t]he one who is able to discern (the real from the unreal), whose mind has developed detachment, who possesses calmness and the allied virtues, and who is longing for liberation, is alone considered qualified to inquire after

Brahman.'[37] Implicit in these verses is that the teaching contained in the body of the work will be fruitful only for those who are qualified in this way.

Closer to our time, we find a similar approach taken by Sri Ramakrishna, the nineteenth-century mystic and saint of Bengal. On several occasions, Sri Ramakrishna spoke about the fitness of an aspirant to reach a spiritual state. To the famous Bengali dramatist Girish Ghosh, he said, "All may wish for such a lofty state, but all cannot attain it. Some bamboos are hollower than others; some are more solid inside."[38] It is said that Sri Ramakrishna's most beloved student, Narendra, would bring all sorts of people to the Master and ask him to bless them. It is not clear that these people had any serious interest in spiritual life. When Sri Ramakrishna would see Narendra approaching, he would sometimes remark, 'What trouble is Narendra bringing today?' The idea is that not everyone is ready to be blessed with spiritual realization. The New Testament says[39] that one should not give what is holy to the dogs or cast pearls before swine.

We caution that none of the above should be understood to mean that some people are destined to realize their potential and that others are not. The difference between a stick of bamboo and a human being is that a bamboo remains the same whereas a human

37 *Vivekachudamani of Sri Sankaracharya*, tr. Swami Madhavananda, 11th edition, Advaita Ashrama, Mayavati, 1982. Note that the translation we give in the text is not exactly that given by Swami Madhavananda, but is an adaptation of it.

38 *Gospel of Sri Ramakrishna*, p. 750. 17th edition.

39 *Matthew*, 7:6

being evolves. We are not the same person we were a year ago, or a week ago. That dynamic aspect is why it is possible to grow, no matter from where one begins. Sri Ramakrishna himself emphasized this point when he said, "The man who says he will never succeed will never succeed. He who feels he is liberated is indeed liberated; and he who feels he is bound verily remains bound. He who forcefully says, 'I am free' is certainly free; and he who says day and night, 'I am bound' is certainly bound."[40]

Whether a person's good wish bears fruit or not depends on both of these conditions being satisfied. Swami Vivekananda speaks about whether the world has any power to affect us. He says that there might be 'microbes of misery' floating around us, but unless we put ourselves in a position that is predisposed to misery, they cannot affect us. Ours is a similar condition with positive wishes, for when we are positioned and predisposed to be a willing receptor of a benevolent wish, we are set up to thrive.

WHAT DO WE REALLY WANT?

From this discussion, we see that in order to best position ourselves to benefit from good wishes, we should ask ourselves this question: what do we really want? Often, we don't know the answer to this question. If we are asked what we want, we might list many things.

40 *Gospel of Sri Ramakrishna*, p. 706.

The next question, then, is why we don't yet have these things. The answer is that in fact we do not really want them. Nothing in the universe can keep us from getting what we intensely want.

We might ask ourselves why it is that some projects remain undone for years, while some projects are completed almost immediately. In one case, either we are not interested or we have convinced ourselves that it cannot be done. Perhaps we ourselves formulated the project. Nevertheless, it is not something that we feel is within our reach. It may be something that we think we 'ought' to be doing, or something that we think the world expects of us. But our heart is not in it. This is why some students seem to be studying diligently but they do not make any progress in their subject.

It is essential to engage in introspection and reflection to ascertain our true desires. A wish will be fruitful only when it addresses something that we intrinsically want as opposed to an ephemeral fancy. Moreover, such a wish will be considered by us as valuable and actionable: acting upon the wish, even if taking a first step forward, will offer us great meaning.

Here, it is important to insert a very important caveat. Among the things that we want, there are some that are good for us, and some that are not. There are some desires that will lead us into a complex and complicated life of obstacles. Being allured by the object of desire, we might not have thought through these complications. If we become aware of all of these, we may no longer be interested in the original object of desire.

Life often presents circumstances as a "package deal." You cannot take one item from the package without taking the entire package.

If we learn to reflect and think seriously about the consequences of what we are reaching for, we will get an idea of the entire package and then be in a better position to decide whether we want all that comes with it. Sometimes we see only a fleeting glimpse of a tip of the iceberg, not even its full tip, realizing that there is a huge mountain of ice submerged that can potentially destroy us.

There is a saying that one should be careful what one wishes for because one is liable to get it. Swami Sarvagatananda always posed the questions, 'What are the consequences? Where does it lead me?' If that is a place you want to be, then embrace this goal.

WHAT IS DESIRE?

It will be useful at this point to discuss the nature of desire according to yoga. What we normally refer to as the mind is better called the inner organ, and it is classified into four functional components. One is the mind itself. This function is the one that determines whether to pay attention or not. A thought or a sensation passes without leaving any impression if we do not pay attention to it. When we use an expression such as 'mind that,' we mean to pay attention to it. When we ask, 'do you mind?' it means 'do you object?' but more abstractly, it means 'is it something that will draw your attention?' When we say, 'Mind your manners,' it means to pay attention to manners. Thus, 'mind' in this sense is a function of paying attention.

The second is *chitta*, or the storage function. There is an accurate record of every thought that we have ever had. It is somewhat incredible to imagine this, since a little reflection will show that we have had billions of thoughts in this life. Assuming we have one thought per second, in 50 years, we will have had 1,576,800,000 thoughts. Perhaps we are inclined to meditation and so we are able to decelerate, to slow down our thoughts for a few hours in the day. But the rest of the time, we may have more than one thought per second as the mind flits from thought to thought with extreme rapidity. The *Isha Upanishad* says that the only thing 'faster' than the mind is consciousness. So, an average estimate of one thought per second is not unreasonable.

Now consider the storage required for these thoughts. Many of these thoughts are in living color so if we were able to store these in physical memory, let us say, conservatively, that one thought takes up about 100 kilobytes of memory. To store all the thoughts that we have had in 50 years would require 157.68 terabytes. With current technology, that amount of storage could be housed in a rack the size of a small bookcase. But we carry that in our head! So, this means that the human being has evolved to create an efficient way of storing and retrieving all of that information.

We know that it is stored because yogis demonstrate that they are able to remember minute details of their life, even from decades earlier.

Each thought is stored with some hooks, and we can think of the hooks as 'metadata.' When a thought is retrieved from memory, it tends to attract or pull up similar, associated thoughts. The similarity is determined by the 'metadata' – in other words, the associations that we have linked to this thought. An objective event can be stored in your mind and in my mind, but the associations that we separately attach to it may be very different. For example, suppose both of us listen to a lecture. For one of us, it may be associated with our days as a student and thinking of this lecture immediately brings to mind memories of our student days. For the other, it may be associated with childhood memories of being lectured to and being told what to do. The objective event is the same but it is recorded and referenced differently according to the individual's experience.

This is why Swami Vivekananda says that when people respond enthusiastically to an idea, it is because they are able to connect it to their own positive experience. This experience might be in the material world or it may be entirely in the psychological world, perhaps a dream or a fantasy. Similarly, when people do not respond to an idea, it suggests that they are not able to relate it to anything that they have experienced before, materially or psychologically, and, as a result, they react with silence, puzzlement, or bewilderment. One often sees these reactions from students. It means that they are missing some prerequisite that we were explicitly or implicitly assuming. At that point, if you are a teacher, you should take a step back, realize that a prerequisite is missing, and address the issue.

The third component of the inner organ is *buddhi*, or the function of decision. How should one react to a thought, if at all? This is determined by the *buddhi.* It also determines whether we should be interested in a thought. These two factors of interest and attention govern the effect of thoughts on our psyche.

The fourth component of the inner organ is *ahamkara*, or the function of identification. To whom do all these thoughts belong? *Ahamkara* is the ego-sense, the sense that declares: 'these are my thoughts.' Both of these functions, namely, decision and identification, add information to the thoughts, or rather to the 'metadata' associated with these thoughts. This 'metadata' affects whether a thought arises in our awareness, or if the ascendance of one thought will trigger the rising of another specific thought. For example, a thought that we strongly identify with will tend to rise more frequently. A collection of thoughts that are similarly labeled will tend to rise simultaneously. This is perhaps a psychological version of the physiological Hebb's law.

A thought stream that is similarly classified becomes a *samskara*, or tendency. When one of these streams comes to the surface, it may influence decisions and identifications. The *buddhi* is likely to pay more attention to a strong thought stream. This then becomes a desire or a wish. The *Gita* says that when we repeatedly think of something, a desire to possess that thing is created.

Even if the *buddhi* is enlightened and informed by other thought streams, and understands that certain of these desires should not be encouraged, there is always the danger that in a particular circumstance, these desires may hold greater sway.

We have many desires. Most of them are just fancies—we have not given them any serious thought. Some of them are deeply ingrained within our psyche. Among these, some are good for us and some are not. A disciplined and well-trained *buddhi* will know the difference. We can develop that capacity through the power of *vicara*, or reflection. Reflection will help us to classify each desire in this way.

It is consequently very important for us to reflect in this way, because suggestions from outside may serve to activate and encourage desires within that are not good for us, and, as in the case of Macbeth, they may lead to disastrous consequences for us and for others. When such suggestions come, we should have a 'not for me' list or a 'not to do' list against which to check their propriety. If the deleterious suggestion appears on that list, we have to put up our defenses.

OUR "NOT TO DO" LIST

When we are able to answer the central concern of the previous section on the nature of fanciful versus ingrained desire, we will understand why some things always remain undone. For it is because we do not really want them to be done. It is better that we recognize that and place them at the top of the list of things not to be done.

Many people have a 'to do' list. But some of us need a 'not to do' list. This list will contain all the things that we thought we wanted to do but have since realized are not for us. By doing this, a significant burden will be lifted from our minds. The anxiety and dissatisfaction associated with having many unfinished projects will melt away. This mental cleansing makes us more effective in going after the pursuits that are core to our being. This is something to keep in mind when we are formulating New Year's resolutions.

It is interesting to note that having a lengthy to-do list is actually a sign of mental dullness. One might believe that being enmeshed in numerous activities is a sign of passion and ambition. But when the list gets too long, it becomes impossible to achieve any of it and this leads to a kind of stupefaction or inertia in which one does not know which of the many undone tasks to take up. Having a long 'to do' list is therefore not a sign of importance or ambition or vision, but rather a sign of dullness, of an inability to prioritize, and an incapacity to match wants with means. The list has to be trimmed down to a manageable size before taking action becomes feasible.

Even if the "to do" list is not too long, it may be unrealistic in other ways. For example, many people include a fitness goal in their New Year's resolutions. The year goes by and they find they have not taken any action related to fitness. This is usually because the goal they had set for themselves is unrealistic. If they are not doing any exercise at the moment and they resolve to exercise for an hour every day, it is very likely that that resolution will be broken. A more realistic resolution may include exercise every other day or exercise for 15 minutes each day.

TIME TO FRUITION

It is difficult to say when a wish will become fruitful. There are some whose good wishes and blessings capture such a broad vision that they do not worry about the time to fruition. They are confident that sooner or later, their thoughts *will* reach fruition, even if it is after centuries. There are some saintly and wise people who enter a cave and emit powerful thoughts and who die in the cave, knowing that their thoughts will continue to reverberate in space until they find a suitable mind to ultimately receive and act upon these expressed thoughts. When a suitable mind is ready to serve as a receptor, the thoughts of these great ones act like a spark, igniting similar or corresponding thoughts in the receptor mind, which, until that point, had lain dormant.

We know the story of Buddha. He was predestined to either be a great king or be a great renunciate and teacher. His father tried his best to keep him in the palace, but once the prince wandered outside the palace, one tour was enough to set his mind into a state of deep contemplation. It is said that he heard some angels singing: "We moan for rest, but rest we can never find . . ." The gist of the song was that all the enjoyments of the world were ephemeral. The story is told to us as the song of some angels. We can understand it as the powerful beneficent thoughts of some ancient sage that found a ready home in the mind of Gautama.

HOW IS IT POSSIBLE?

How is it possible for good wishes to have an effect even when they are not expressed in words and even when we are not physically in contact with the individual we are trying to help? According to Swami Vivekananda, "This mind is a part of the universal mind. Each mind is connected with every other mind. And each mind, wherever it is located, is in actual communication with the whole world."[41]

He also says, "The world is one of influence. Part of our energy is used up in the preservation of our own bodies. Beyond that, every

41 "The powers of the mind," in: *Complete Works*, Volume 2, pp. 12–13.

particle of our energy is day and night being used in influencing others. Our bodies, our virtues, our intellect, and our spirituality, all these are continually influencing others; and so, conversely, we are being influenced by them."[42]

This influence comes to us as a suggestion. That is why we need to cultivate a regular practice of reflection. All of these suggestions that are consciously or unconsciously planted in the mind have to be examined. Most of them are not relevant to us and so should be uprooted and rejected. Some may seem relevant, but even they have to be placed in the context of our overall trajectory and personal priorities, and if they do not fit, they also should be rejected.

We should also examine our overall trajectory. Where is it leading us? Is that a place we want to be? We tend to underestimate the influence that is exerted on us by the world, but we do so to our detriment. After visiting a place, if we sit quietly and observe the mind, we find that the thoughts that are flowing are related to that place. And that is only what is on the surface. It is quite possible that the place has dealt other effects upon us that we are not able to detect right away. Regular reflection is necessary to see that these kinds of influences do not harm our mental health, just as regular bathing is needed to make sure that microbes do not negatively affect our bodily health.

42 "The powers of the mind," in: *Complete Works*, Volume 2, p. 13.

HOW ARE GOOD WISHES SENT?

They could be verbal or written, as when we greet someone or when we send a greeting card. But there are many other ways to send good wishes. Some of these are considerably subtler and, with subtlety, more powerful. Immense power is in the subtle.

We need not be in contact with the person to whom we aim to send good wishes. However, our mind should be prepared. One good method to prepare the mind is to adopt a prayerful attitude. When the mind is collected and in a devotional mood, then one may picture the individual or the circumstance that we wish to affect. If someone is in trouble, we can offer that person and their trouble to our chosen ideal of beneficence, and we can pray that this individual be taken care of. Or we may imagine that person in better circumstances where they have overcome the difficulty currently facing them. Strong imagination is very powerful in purposefully creating this reality.

In all these methods, one factor that is common and which plays a significant role in determining whether our good wishes actually benefit the individual is the extent to which we are unselfish. If we are doing this with any selfish motive whatsoever, our prayer may be misguided. One who sends good wishes with no selfish or ulterior motive is likely to succeed. In fact, for good wishes to be effective, the sole intention should be the genuine desire for the recipient's well-being.

Swami Vivekananda wrote to his brother disciples, some of whom were suffering from various kinds of ailments. He wrote, "Why are Baburam and Yogen suffering so much? It is owing to their negative, their self-abasing spirit." He further instructed them to reflect for an hour at a stretch that, as embodiments of consciousness, they cannot be affected by disease. Such reflection, he said, would result in a manifestation of strength and well-being. He also asked all of them to think in this way, not only for themselves, but also in reference to everyone else in the group.

Swami Vivekananda is not the first or the only teacher to suggest that our thoughts can yield a physical effect. We find this in both ancient and contemporary teaching, and in both eastern and western thought. Nevertheless, we seem to be quick to forget it and so it bears frequent repetition.[43]

DEALING WITH BAD WISHES

Whenever we discuss good wishes, we have also to deal with the opposite, namely, malevolent wishes. It is important to be able to recognize good and bad wishes, whether they arise from within ourselves or whether others are sending us such wishes. Let us briefly discuss what we might term as 'bad wishes.' By this we mean unhealthy, destructive, and negative wishes. How do we deal with bad wishes brewing within ourselves?

We have already discussed how we should use reflection to weed out the desires that may not be good for us. Of course, this is

43 See, for example, Joe Dispenza, *You Are the Placebo: Making Your Mind Matter*, Hay House Inc., 2015.

more easily said than done and anyone who is serious about it will need to think through what action steps they will take to achieve this. Key for any such set of actions to be successful is desire itself, namely, the desire to master that which is not good for us.[44] The same process can be used to neutralize or minimize the effect of negative ways of thinking.

How do we deal with bad wishes of others directed toward us? The negative thoughts that come to us from others should also be neutralized. In the first place, there may be an objective cause for them, and, if possible, we should try to address that. If we made a mistake, it is better to acknowledge it and correct it if possible. Though painful in the short term, in the long term it is very beneficial for us.

But this is by far the *easiest* aspect to deal with. More difficult is the emotional and irrational aspects that often accompany negative thoughts. In this case, prayer and forbearance are the only tools we have. Christ said, 'Bless them that curse you.' We have to pray for them. And Buddha said that hatred is never cured by hatred, but by love alone. If we don't introduce the positive thoughts, our mind will become disturbed and we will only add to the pool of negative thoughts. Rather, we should entertain thoughts that will neutralize the negative thoughts that are 'in the air.' This may be difficult, but it is not impossible.

44 Sri Ramakrishna had a saying that to remove a thorn that has pierced one's foot, one needs another thorn.

We should remember that we live in a world of cause and effect. Some reflection will convince us that behind the events of the world are the thoughts of people. People are a combination of many factors, both good and bad. Those who think ill of us may have some very positive qualities. Remembering these can mollify one's anger. Also, for those who believe in God, we should remember that God is the final arbiter and that all things happen by God's will.

The one who has not learnt the art of forbearance will perish. Forbearance is not a sign of weakness. Everyone knows how to become angry. It is in fact a sign of great inner strength to be able to restrain that emotion.

We should ask ourselves why we should place our mental peace and our happiness in the hands of anyone other than ourselves. That is only a recipe for unhappiness. Also, we should try, as far as possible, to be positive and behave in a proper manner even with those who wish ill of us. It is not easy to do, but it is important to make the effort. Why should anyone have the power to remove the smile from my face, or from yours?

IMPLICATIONS FOR CONDUCT

We have seen that good wishes arouse something within ourselves that helps us to realize our goal. We have to practice reflection in order to understand what our intrinsic desires are, to refine and prioritize our goals and even to remove some of them from our list. If we want to help others through good wishes, it can only be on the basis of unselfish love. Holy Mother said that if we want peace of mind, we should not find fault with others. She went on to say, 'make everyone your own.' Certainly, we want good things for 'our own,' so that means we should send good wishes to everyone. There are no enemies and no strangers. Good wishes do not mean that we should encourage everything that someone is doing. We should wish for the well-being of that person, with no selfish or ulterior motive in our wish. Then that wish will be fruitful and will lead to the true well-being of the individual. This, in turn, leads to a society and a world of people who are more at peace with themselves and this process will thus propagate world peace. What was intended as a good wish for one person actually becomes a blessing to humanity. That is why we often pray, '*sarve jana sukhino bhavanthu; samastha sammangalo nisanthu.*' That is, may all be happy and may good things come to everyone. This is the best good wish, the wish that matters most.

3

THANK YOU

INTRODUCTION

THE TITLE OF this chapter – "Thank you" – may seem a little strange and so let me begin by saying a few words by way of explanation.[45] When I first contemplated this topic and its connectivity to the science of human possibilities, American Thanksgiving had been around the corner, so it seemed a good time to reflect on what it is we have to be thankful for, and why gratitude matters to ennobling the human mind. Also, we were close to the birth anniversary of Swami Sarvagatananda.

For about 40 years (from 1962 to 2001) Swami Sarvagatananda was the monk in charge of both the Ramakrishna Vedanta Society

45 Based on a talk at the Ramakrishna Vedanta Society of Massachusetts and the Vedanta Society of Providence on Sunday, November 13, 2011.

of Massachusetts in Boston, as well as the Vedanta Society of Providence, Rhode Island. He had arrived in America in 1954 as the assistant Swami at both Societies, and was appointed the head on the passing of his predecessor Swami Akhilananda. Since 1954, Swami was also the Hindu Chaplain at MIT and would come to campus weekly to speak with students and faculty. He would normally be at the Chaplain's office near the MIT Chapel.

As a teacher of Vedanta, Swami had many original and unique insights that made conversations with him so fascinating. During the time we were graduate students, I, along with my brother Ram and our friend, Cyrus Mehta, used to meet Swami at MIT in his Chaplain's Office every Friday afternoon and spend several hours in discussion about Vedanta.

Many years later, I came to know that the mathematician Norbert Wiener followed a similar practice. According to the biography of Wiener by Flo Conway and Jim Siegelman, "The Swami came to MIT on Fridays, and Wiener paid a visit to him in the chapel's counseling office almost every week." It was a bit unusual because Wiener was a self-declared agnostic, but he was fascinated by Swami's description of reincarnation. In fact, they discussed many topics including the impact that the computer revolution would have on humanity. Swami describes Wiener as "somber and filled with foreboding" that this new technology would obscure the real needs of humanity. But Wiener also had a playful side, announcing himself as 'Swami's bearded student' and when he came to Swami's office, they would spend the whole day together gripped in conversation. Amar Bose, a junior colleague of Wiener at MIT, who went on to found the Bose Corporation in 1964, also used to meet

Swami and had heard of 'a bearded student' but had no idea that it was Wiener. Bose remarks that "in hindsight, he could see some flickers of a spiritual side emerging among Wiener's many facets."[46]

Wiener and Bose are well-known figures, but I wonder how many generations of students benefited from Swami's presence at the chaplain's office over the several decades that he was there. Certainly for me, I don't think it is an exaggeration to say that those conversations essentially formed the basis of my understanding of Vedanta and that they shaped the outlook on life and on human possibilities expressed in these pages.

Besides his philosophical and spiritual insights, Swami was also a very loving person, and even a casual visitor could feel that love. I think he touched many lives through his affectionate concern for people. So many people felt thankful to have his company. Perhaps that is why it became a tradition to observe his birthday on Thanksgiving Day.

Swami said that when he first came to America, two things caught his attention and appreciation. One was the way people said 'thank you' to each other, even for trivial things. The second was the hospitals of America. Having spent some of his most spiritually formative years in Kankhal (near the famous holy city of Hardhwar) in charge of the hospital there, he appreciated how well organized the hospitals were in America and how well the patients were taken care of. Of course, that was in the 1950s and things have changed

46 Flo Conway and Jim Siegelman, *Dark Hero of the Information Age: In Search of Norbert Wiener, the Father of Cybernetics*, pp. 307-310, Basic Books, New York, 2005.

quite a bit in that regard. Nevertheless, this is the background for my choosing the title of this chapter.

In discussing thankfulness, I am not going to take the approach of 'praising the Lord.' That is a very difficult approach I think. If we want to praise the Lord, we should be ready to offer praise for everything: failure, as well as for success, for poverty as well as for wealth, for disease as well as for health, and for grief as well as for happiness. In order to really be able to do that, we would have to be quite mature from a spiritual point of view.

Fundamental to a spiritual point of view is to realize that life is a process of growth and learning. If we can take the position of a student and view everything as a teaching, then we will be able to benefit from failure as well as success, from poverty as well as wealth, from disease as well as health, and from grief as well as from happiness.[47] The student-teacher relationship allows us to be thankful about everything because everything contains some wisdom or some teaching. Uncovering that wisdom propels us forward in terms of growth and spiritual evolution. But it may be very hard to do in practice.

If we are not ready yet to view God as teacher, we can begin instead with our human teachers, and that is the perspective that I will take. This perspective also has the advantage that it does

47 Swami Vivekananda writes: "After a time, man finds that it is not happiness, but knowledge, towards which he is going, and that both pleasure and pain are great teachers, and that he learns as much from evil as from good" (*Complete Works*, Volume 1, p. 27).

not depend on our belief in God. It is as relevant to atheists and agnostics as it is to believers. Life is a process of learning and growth for all of us.

THANKFULNESS AND APPRECIATION

If our mind is open, we can learn from everything and everyone around us. There is the famous phrase, 'books in brooks, sermons in stones and good in everything.' Sri Ramakrishna exuded this attitude that he could learn from everything. One of his aphoristic statements was '*yavat bachi, tavat shikhi*' – as long as I live, so long do I learn. He would himself go, even uninvited, if he heard that someone was living a spiritual life. He would go there with utmost respect and ask the person about their views on God and spiritual matters. He even looked at a dog and wondered what he might learn from the dog. His humility is truly charming, and one cannot help but be touched by it when reading about his life and teachings.

The challenge, then, is to be able to steady our mind in a positive, receptive, and open state. This is where thankfulness can be a great help. Whenever we say 'thank you,' we are expressing appreciation. Of course, sometimes, people say 'thank you' or 'thanks a lot' when they mean exactly the opposite.[48] It depends on their inflection.

48 In his essay "Politics and the English Language," published in 1946, George Orwell criticized the use of stale and overused language in political discourse, referring to it as "hackneyed phrases." Here, we are referring to sincerely expressed gratitude.

Most often, 'thank you' is an expression of appreciation, and our mind will be open to the teaching around us if we consciously learn to be more appreciative.

In a financial context, the word 'appreciate' means to increase in value. From one point of view, the thing or person held in appreciation is increasing in value in our estimation. But from another, deeper point of view, it is *we ourselves* who increase in value. For we are the ones who benefit because our mind now finds itself in a positive and receptive state that coats a thing or person with the value it merits.

Thankfulness and appreciation is a very important topic because it figures into our daily interactions. Most of our day is spent in interacting with people and so if we can set that in proper order, and understand what acts or expressions are additive in value, then this understanding can be immediately beneficial to advancing the science of human possibilities. But in order to reach this understanding, we have to pay close attention to what transpires in daily living.

We find in many places, for example, people who are unable or unwilling to communicate with one another. They get on each other's nerves and are not able to do anything cooperatively. These people may smile at each other perfunctorily and even speak politely, but still they are not able to cooperate meaningfully in any endeavor. What is the cause of this? The cause of all this is their negative estimation of the other, and this renders ineffective all of their good intentions.

This suggests that if we want to be able to cooperate creatively or constructively with people, we must begin with a basic respect or appreciation for the other person as a person. As we each have our idiosyncrasies, and as we loathe giving them up, we must also understand that others are in a similar situation.

From one point of view, the idiosyncrasies of any person are in fact what make that person beautiful. It is their uniqueness. You might recall having seen flowers that mesmerize you? How many different kinds there are! Each has its own charm and beauty. The beauty of a rose cannot be the beauty of a hibiscus. Can you say which is more beautiful? No, you really cannot. You may have a preference for one or the other for various reasons, but that does not diminish from the beauty of the less preferred flower in any way. Swami Sarvagatananda used to say that all flowers are the smile of the Divine Mother. What a captivating and highly evocative description! Our view of flowers will never be the same again.

At one time, Sri Ramakrishna went to the garden to gather flowers for worship in the temple. As he was about to start, he had a vision that worship had already been completed and that the flowers on the trees and shrubs, paragons of beauty, had already been offered to the Divine Being manifested in nature. He could not therefore pick the flowers. The flowers were perfectly arranged just as they were.

There is a similar incident described in a famous Telugu poem. A devotee comes to the temple and starts speaking to the Deity: "I am sorry but I don't have any flowers to offer. I went to the garden to pick them, when one of the flowers started scolding me in a tiny voice. It said: 'born in the land of Buddha, you want to do violence to us. You will break our neck and put a pin in it and call it a garland. How can any god be happy with such an offering? What heartless creatures human beings are!' Scolded in this way, I could not pick any of the flowers!"[49] These kinds of insights, original and deep, are only possible to a mind that is receptive and appreciative of beauty in all its forms.

Returning to the rose, if we appreciate the rose, we must also appreciate the thorns. A rose would not be a rose without its thorns. I am not saying that we praise the thorns. But understand that they are there and that is a fact and that is just the way it is. Appreciate them to that extent. Many things in life are like the rose. Beautiful, but also jagged. In Swami Vivekananda's poem 'The Cup,' the Divine Mother says, 'I made the stones that cut your feet. I don't ask you to understand. I only ask you to come unto Me.'[50]

Like roses, a similar phenomenon arises with people. We may have a preference for certain kinds of character but we cannot condemn anyone for their idiosyncrasies. For example, some people are very particular about rituals: everything has to be done just right. And so, if we have to work with such a person, then everything better be done just right, or, in any case, we have to try our best to do everything just right. It is not the time to give them a lecture on how rituals might be stunting our growth or how we should go beyond rituals or any such thing.

What exists in the world are not abstract principles and ideologies, but living beings each possessed of imperfections. Living beings

49 This is from the poem *Pushpa vilaapam* or the 'The Lament of the Flowers' by Jandhyala Paapayya Sastry.

50 *Complete Works*, Volume 6, p. 177.

are a composite of so many things: good, bad and indifferent. Just as a rose is the beautiful flower and the prickly thorns, people are basically good but they come individually gift-wrapped, as it were, enveloped with all sorts of idiosyncrasies. And there are no exceptions. Saints have idiosyncrasies and sinners have idiosyncrasies. The wealthy have idiosyncrasies, and the poor have idiosyncrasies. These are simply a function of body and mind.

We should not, therefore, be thrown off balance by these idiosyncrasies, otherwise we will miss something important. Once someone came to the monastery at Belur to see Swami Brahmananda.[51] He found him with a group of visitors engaged in some light talk, perhaps about food. The person thought, 'this is a saint? He is more occupied with getting good food!' and he left. Some people may try to see something deep in Swami Brahmananda's discussion of food, but I would say it is just an idiosyncrasy. Had the visitor stayed and allowed for the conversation to finish, and had he asked Swami Brahmananda a question about spiritual life, he could have received a response of great help to him.

To separate out the idiosyncrasies from the essential core requires us to practice some *viveka*, or discernment. Discernment is the ability to tease out the different strands that make a composite. Its opposite is confusion, where we lump everything together. In the literature, we often see *viveka* translated as 'discrimination.'

51 Swami Brahmananda was a direct disciple of Sri Ramakrishna and was considered second only to Swami Vivekananda in terms of spiritual insight and attainment. He was the first president of the Ramakrishna Math (Monastery) and Mission.

It seems to me this is not accurate. The difference between the two is that discrimination is discernment together with a value judgment. Discernment by itself is neutral and does not involve any judgment. What we want is the ability to separate the different strands and to focus on what will be beneficial for us, with no value judgment about other things. Regarding the other things, we should be ready to say 'I don't know.'

This is something Swami Sarvagatananda used to tell us quite often. We can ask why someone said or did something, yet, most of the time, the answer will be that we just don't know. And because of that uncertainty as to cause and effect, we have to be very careful about trying to set anyone right. The chances that we have completely misunderstood the situation are quite high.

In trying to practice this kind of thankfulness and awareness, there are some dangers that we should be aware of. Firstly, it does not mean that we become a doormat for everyone. It does not mean that we have to compromise our values or principles or abandon our reason. In this regard, Sri Ramakrishna gives several parables.

The first is about the snake that wanted to live a spiritual life. Once, a very poisonous snake lived in a certain meadow and now and then, it would slither furtively out of its hole and scare the people in that area, mostly boys who were tending their flocks of cattle. One day, a holy man was walking through the area when the boys noticed it and warned him about the nearby snake. He calmly said that he was not worried and that he could protect himself. So, he continued along, and soon enough the snake challenged him. Uttering some *mantras*, he sprinkled some water on the snake and it instantly lost its ferocity and lay harmless at his feet.

Then he asked the snake, 'why do you scare people like that?' The snake replied: 'like what? I'm a snake. That's what snakes do.' The holy man said, 'No, that is not good. I will teach you a *mantra* and repeating this, you will realize God. And from now on, you must give up doing harm to anyone.' So, the snake was initiated with a *mantra* and after the holy man departed, it started its *sadhana* (spiritual practice).

In time, the boys came to realize that the snake was no longer threatening them, so, summoning courage, they started to throw stones at it. As it tried to escape, they grew bolder still, and one of them picked it up by the tail and whirled it around and slapped it on the ground until it was unconscious. They left it there assuming it to be dead. However, it wasn't dead. Much later, the snake regained consciousness and sluggishly made its way home, eventually burrowing back into its hole. It survived by only coming out of its hole at night.

Months later, when the holy man again passed through that same way, he asked the boys where the snake was. They said that it had died long ago, but he did not believe them. He was confident that the *mantra* he had given the snake would bear fruit and that it would realize God. He went out into the meadow and called out to the snake by the name that he had given it. Hearing its teacher's voice, the snake emerged from the hole and slithered toward the feet of the holy man. He was shocked to see the snake's emaciated condition, and, upon hearing all that had transpired, he asked the snake why it had not defended itself. The snake said: 'Holy sir, you asked me to give up violence.' To this the saint replied, 'I asked you not to bite anyone. I did not ask you not to hiss. You could have hissed to protect yourself.'

This story contains several important lessons. Firstly, appreciate everyone but protect yourself. This is because we are also included in 'everyone'. Swami Sarvagatananda told us a story of a person who was walking on the beach, enjoying the air and twirling his cane. There was another person walking behind. The cane was coming dangerously close to him so he called out to the man ahead: 'Hey Mister, stop twirling your cane.' The man replied, 'It's a free beach. I can twirl my cane if I want to.' At this, the second man said, 'Your freedom ends where my nose begins.' Appreciate everyone – even yourself. We have to appreciate ourselves as well. We shall return to this concept of self-appreciation a little later in this book.

It bears noting here that an enlightened teacher can assist us in transcending our idiosyncrasies. We see this transcendence in a very highly developed form in Sri Ramakrishna. From Swami Vivekananda's account, Sri Ramakrishna had the ability to literally 'see' the future potential of a person and would hold that exalted image in front of them and guide them forward accordingly. In his eyes, that potential precluded him from condemning anyone for their present weaknesses. It did not prevent him, however, from helping them to correct those present deficiencies, but it was done in the light of this very hopeful future. In his essay, "My Master,"[52] Vivekananda describes how he would encourage even those people whom others considered worthless and how he never had a word of condemnation for any.

52 *Complete Works*, Volume 4, pp. 154-187. This essay is based on two talks given by Swami Vivekananda in 1896.

However, we are not Ramakrishna. We should know our strengths. The chances of our being able to give a different direction to someone's life, to help them to go beyond their idiosyncrasies, are quite small. The better way is to pray quietly for them and speak in positive and encouraging words. During his initial encounter with Sri Ramakrishna, his disciple Mahendranath Gupta (referred to as M) humbly questions whether it would be appropriate to educate individuals that the clay image in the temple is not God. At that time, there were several movements in India such as the Brahmo Samaj expressing the view that image worship was a superstition and that people had to be enlightened about this. Sri Ramakrishna scolded him: 'That's the trouble with you Calcutta people. You are always trying to enlighten others without thinking of how to get the light yourself. Firstly, it is not an image of clay, but an image of spirit (what a beautiful phrase!). Secondly, even if the worship is mistaken, do you think that God cannot teach them and that He is waiting for your help?'[53]

A devotee of Sri Ramakrishna in Toronto told me a story of a priest in a temple who tended to be very grouchy. He would snarl and scowl at the devotees. It was so noticeable that people were starting to complain, she told me. But instead of complaining, she went up to him and said, 'you look so nice when you smile.' That compliment made him smile. On the other hand, if we had gone and lectured him on the importance of not being grouchy in a

53 The complete conversation is described in the *Gospel of Sri Ramakrishna*, pp. 79-83. The segment described in the text occurs on p. 80.

place of worship, it is not clear that we would have made much progress.

Another story told by Sri Ramakrishna is about the '*mahut Narayana.*' Once there was a school in which the day's lesson was that God dwells in all beings. Later that day, the students went to the village to gather alms. Suddenly, there was a commotion and a wild elephant was charging directly toward where the student was standing. The *mahut* (the person trying to drive the elephant) was yelling that the elephant was out of control, that it was a mad elephant and that people should get out of the way. But the student began to reason: 'the elephant is also God, so why should I move?' The elephant picked up the boy with its trunk and flung him aside. Later the teacher and the brother disciples came looking for this student, and, finding him unconscious, took him back to the school and nursed him back to health. Then the teacher asked him why he did not get out of the way of the elephant. The student replied that, as the elephant was God, he did not see the need for moving. The teacher asked, 'but why did you not listen to the Mahut God who was telling you to get out of the way?' If the elephant is God, then the mahut is also God!

The mad elephant of the story is a manifestation of God, but so is the *mahut* who is telling us to get out of the elephant's path! Spiritual life does not contradict our intelligence or reason, but rather fulfills it. We should not abandon reason, but allow it to mature and grow with the help of our creative and spiritual insights. If we keep this in mind, we will not be in danger when we try to practice being appreciative and thankful.

APPRECIATING OURSELVES

According to Vedanta psychology, what we see outside is but a reflection of what is within. Negative attitudes projected outside arise from negative attitudes about ourselves. Appreciation of external others has to be rooted in an appreciation of ourselves. Moreover, this appreciation has to be based not on comparison to others but on an understanding and appreciation of the way things are.

In his essay "Self-Reliance," the philosopher and essayist Ralph Waldo Emerson, writes, "There is a time in every man's education when he arrives at the conviction that envy is ignorance; that imitation is suicide; that he must take himself for better, for worse, as his portion; that though the wide universe is full of good, no kernel of nourishing corn can come to him but through his toil bestowed on that plot of ground which is given to him to till." We have to be comfortable with ourselves. And only that which we ourselves struggle for and work for will be ours. Nor can we possibly accelerate our innate strengths and contributions to this world if we are not comfortable in our own skin and minds.

To be comfortable with ourselves does not mean that we think everything is okay and there is nothing left to do. It means that the basis of our appreciation of ourselves lies deeper than our thoughts and actions. Our body is constantly changing, our thoughts are constantly changing, but we are greater than their sum. In fact, a definition of spirit is that which is not matter and not mind, and we are the embodiments of spirit.

Even if we don't want to acknowledge or use the word 'spirit,' our common experience tells us that the individual is greater than his or her thoughts and actions. And this experience is called love. When parents love their children, it is not on the basis of achievement. They love them just for being who they are. That suggests that even in common experience, we acknowledge that a person is more than her thoughts and actions. If we don't want to use the word 'spirit,' then we may use the word 'love.' When we are conscious of the love that is within us, the love that we express to others and others express to us, then we find that we become very comfortable with ourselves. In so doing, the science of human possibilities finds us, and we navigate toward it excitedly.

If we identify ourselves with our thoughts and actions, there is a lot to correct. At first, one might be a little despondent. When we begin to examine ourselves, we might see more negative than positive. But that just means that there is no time to lose! Swami Sarvagatananda used to say, 'No case is hopeless, never is it too late.'

In the process of spiritual growth, we cannot ever give up or allow ourselves to become despondent. It is not only spiritual growth, but growth in general that we must pursue with tenacity. The journey of a thousand miles begins with the first step. With each step, we move toward the goal. Every step taken toward the east puts us a step further from the west. And even in the journey, there may be setbacks, backslidings, and stumbles. Swami Vivekananda said that the sign of greatness is not that we never fall down, but that we get up each time and continue the march.

It is very important to understand that appreciating ourselves cannot be on the basis of comparison or on the basis of achievement. If we compare ourselves with others, we will always feel unsatisfied. We will not rise to fulfill the possibility that resides within each of us. There is the story of a person who felt he had an inferiority complex. He went to see a psychiatrist and they had many sessions where the patient related everything about himself and his troubles to the psychiatrist. At the end of the therapy session, the psychiatrist said, 'I am happy to tell you that you do not in fact have an inferiority complex. You are simply inferior!' Needless to say, that was not very helpful!

The reality is that there will always be those who are better than us, and those who are not as good as we are, whatever the skill may be. Still, each of us has a contribution to make. This kind of idea is beautifully depicted in the *Katha Upanishad*. The young boy, *Nachiketas*, thinks to himself about the question of death and resolves that he will discover the answer to what happens after death. He tells himself, 'Amongst many, I am among the top. Amongst others, I am in the middle' and with that confidence resolves that he will solve the problem of whether any aspect of the individual survives physical death.'

And with that attitude of *shraddha* (which can be roughly translated as faith in himself) he went forward to realize his goal. That is a beautiful story because it is a positive feeling that we know where we stand and we know that we have a contribution to make concerning this problem. It is a very inspiring story. We don't whitewash our weaknesses and pretend they don't exist. We take stock of who and what we are and try to move forward from there.

Faith in oneself was also a keynote of Vivekananda's message. To quote his own words, "To preach the doctrine of *shraddha* or genuine faith is the mission of my life. Let me repeat to you that this faith is one of the potent factors of humanity and of all religions. First have faith in yourselves."

The Gita says, "Let a man raise himself by himself. Let him not drag himself down. For he himself is his own friend and he himself is his own enemy." With this attitude, we have a good mindset for creative activity.

Again, to quote Emerson: "A man should learn to detect and watch that gleam of light which flashes across his mind from within, more than the luster of the firmament of bards and sages. Yet he dismisses without notice his thought, because it is his. In every work of genius, we recognize our own rejected thoughts: they come back to us with a certain alienated majesty. Great works of art have no more affecting lesson for us than this. They teach us to abide by our spontaneous impression with good-humored inflexibility then most when the whole cry of voices is on the other side. Else, tomorrow, a stranger will say with masterly good sense precisely what we have thought and felt all the time, and we shall be forced to take with shame, our own opinion from another."

If appreciating others without appreciating ourselves is a pitfall, so is the reverse. However, in general, both can be practiced properly only when they are practiced together. A person who has faith in himself or herself will also have faith in others. A person who truly has strength will have faith in the strength of others. Where we see a person who exudes self-confidence and strength, but who doesn't have confidence in the strength of others, we actually have reason to be suspicious. Underlying this apparent strength, there may be a serious weakness afoot. And when that is uncovered, it will be a great blow to the individual. On the other hand, without uncovering it, that individual cannot really progress and grow as a person.

We are in a symbiotic relationship with the world. We affect the world and it affects us. Our attitudes about the world and our attitudes about ourselves have, of a necessity, to be related. A person who is too critical of the world is probably too critical of himself or herself also. This is why Swami Sarvagatananda taught us the prayer, 'May I not accuse, demand or complain, but love, respect and cooperate with all.'

Swami told us the story of a secretary at MIT who was having problems with her staff. He told her to place a sign on her desk: 'No ADC.' This was a mnemonic for 'accuse, demand, complain.' She tried that for one week and found that it actually helped. Then he told her the second week to place a sign on her desk: 'LRC,' a mnemonic for 'love, respect, cooperate.' The staff became much more cooperative when they observed the change. First, eliminate the obvious negative things and then start emphasizing the positive. In practice, we may not be able to separate it out like that: usually, we take a combined approach.

It is a myth to think that denouncing someone or something will edify us. When we see such towering spiritual personalities as Sri Ramakrishna not having a word of condemnation for anyone, then I wonder how we dare to be so self-righteous. Really, if we read the lives of the great spiritual giants, we find them to be wonderfully compassionate and understanding. And 'thank you,' the focus of this chapter, is an attempt to bring some of that into our own lives and into our spiritual practice.

Let us explore a little more of this psychology, which will take our accusing finger and eventually point it back at ourselves. Sri Sarada Devi taught, "If you want peace of mind, my child, do not find the faults of others. Rather, learn to find your own faults. No one is a stranger my child. Learn to make all your own. The world is your own." The psychology behind this is explained by another story of Sri Ramakrishna.

Sri Ramakrishna compares the mind to a white cloth, which takes the color of whatever dye it is dipped into. The cloth is our mind and the dye is the set of thoughts that we entertain. If we dwell on something negative, the mind becomes colored with that negativity. If we enumerate the faults of others, what we are doing is dyeing our mind in the color of those faults. In other words, we are taking on the nature of what we are condemning. Swami Sarvagatananda used to say, 'There is dirt on the road. So why should you pick it up and put it into your pocket?' And again, to quote the Holy Mother: "Man finds faults in others often bringing down his mind to that level. Does anyone really lose anything by others' criticism? The critic himself suffers."

On the other hand, if we dwell on the positive, our mind is colored with positivity. This is why we seek holy company. The holiness that we see in their behavior starts to get reflected on us. There is a beautiful story in the *Upanishads* of two birds perched on a fruit tree. One bird is sitting at the top, calm and resplendent. The other bird is lower down the tree. It begins to eat the fruit, some sweet and some bitter. Occasionally, especially when it bites into a bitter fruit, it looks up at the peaceful and luminous bird. Being attracted it comes closer, but is then again distracted by the fruits. In this way, coming closer and closer, it finds at a certain point that the rays of light surrounding the calm bird start to be reflected upon itself as well.

BE POSITIVE AND NEVER COMPLAIN

Once, a devotee asked Swami Sarvagatananda about the attitude with which one should serve in the Vedanta Society. His reply was, 'be positive and never complain.' It seems to me that this is extremely valuable advice. For the most part, our understanding is quite limited, and with that limited understanding we try to evaluate others and their actions. Inevitably, we will find their actions wanting and full of shortcomings. As a result, we will start complaining and becoming negative about things and people.

It seems to me that Vedanta is sort of like nuclear energy. It is so powerful that it is difficult to contain it and difficult to work with it. In this case, the spent fuel is the ego. It is toxic and one should limit one's exposure to it. In the physical world, we still don't know how to deal with the dangers posed by spent fuel, yet in the spiritual realm, we have been given a solution. You can't get rid of the ego, but you can 'ripen it' as Sri Ramakrishna says. You can broaden it and divinize it, and then it becomes harmless.

In actual fact, the study and practice of Vedanta forces us to grow and one has to be ready for that maturation. Growth always challenges the status quo. If we are neither ready, nor able to digest that, there will be a struggle. As a result, we may become a little irascible and as a result start to see things and people in a negative light. We might find that we are not able to deal with the change in ourselves. But instead of pointing the figure inwards, we point it outward. So goes our thinking: 'There is something wrong with all of you and if you would just behave well, I would be all right.'

When we feel such things happening, it is a good idea to take a step back and slow the pace a little bit until we reach a comfort level. There is no point in rushing forward at a speed that we cannot sustain comfortably. We must behold that an inexorable change is happening within us. If we can keep an alert and mindful attitude, we will see that. Being positive and never complaining is itself a spiritual practice that can hasten our spiritual growth.

In explaining the various disciplines that help us advance in spiritual life, or even in life in general, Swami Vivekananda had a broad classification of the four yogas. *Jnana yoga* is an approach that emphasizes philosophy and the exercise of reason. *Bhakti yoga* is an approach that emphasizes the power of emotion and devotion. *Raja yoga* is a psychological approach that emphasizes the mind and its control. *Karma yoga* is an approach that emphasizes action and teaches us how to use action as a means to spiritual growth. Swami Sarvagatananda used to say that any of the yogas by themselves will take us to the realization of spirit. But of all the yogas, *Karma yoga* is potentially the 'fastest.' The catch, however, is that in order to sustain that, we have to be able to take care of our ego. It will get very bruised and even injured and will demand our attention. If we can wrest it under control, or, rather, if we can win its cooperation, then we will move forward at a very fast speed. The tendency to be negative and to complain is our ego trying to reassert itself.

BE ALERT AND BE MINDFUL

In theory, this prescription to be alert and mindful may sound obvious, but in practice, all of this may not be so clear. We may not even be aware what kind of thoughts we are collecting in our mind. This is why we require introspection and contemplation. And so, we need to be in a state of constant alertness and mindfulness. Alert mindfulness, as Swami Sarvagatananda used to say, will help us to guide ourselves properly. And we need to think before we act: 'Where does this lead me? What are the consequences?'

All of this discussion finally returns us to spiritual appreciation. The *Isha Upanishad* says that the Divine substance is present in every aspect of existence, even in the very minutest portion. The God of the Upanishads, of Vedanta, is not unrelated to our present existence or experience. Nor is it an extra cosmic God, which intervenes in this world to help some and punish others. It is Being, It is awareness, and It is love. And when It is seen on the plane of matter, that is, through the mind and the senses, It appears as the world. If and when we transcend mind and senses, as saints and sages throughout the ages have done, this very world will be seen as the Divine substance and that is the state of *Jivanmukta*.

But even if we have not reached that state, that level of experience, if we can get some sort of intellectual conviction in it, we can take it as a philosophical basis for the way we look at things and people and ourselves. The *Gita* expresses this in the following way: "Whatever being there is glorious, prosperous or powerful, know that to have sprung from a spark of My splendor." Swami Vivekananda takes this one step further. God is not only where there is intelligence, but also where there is stupidity; not only where there is wealth, but also where there is poverty; not only where there is health, but also where there is disease. This idea is also in the *Gita* but not quoted as often: "Everywhere His hands, everywhere His face, everywhere His feet." In Swami Vivekananda's words, "And above all, my God the poor, my God the wretched, my God the sick shall be the special object of my worship."

Notice that when seen in this light, it is not a matter of being compassionate to fellow human beings, but worshipping them as Gods through service. And now you see this has tremendous consequences, because it deifies everything. And this is the real basis of appreciation. Acknowledging the underlying divinity of everything is the real basis of 'thank you.' And so to you, dear reader, I say, "Thank you!"

4

HOW TO STUDY

THE QUESTION OF how to study presupposes the answers to two other questions: first, what do we mean by study, and second, why do we need to study?

The word 'study' is used both as a noun and as a verb. In the social sciences, it is used as a noun to signify a method of establishing in a systematic way an empirical basis for a certain policy or position. In the medical sciences, it is similarly used as a noun to validate a certain medication or a method of treatment. Here, however, we use it as a verb, which represents a method of acquiring knowledge.

Those who are studying are called students. In the fourfold Vedic division of life, student life is the first. It is called *brahmacharya*. From there one moves on to *grhastha*, or the life of the householder. That transition signifies a formal end to student life. However, the transition does not mean that we can stop learning. In fact, learning is a lifelong process. It is in this sense that it is said that student life has a beginning but no ending.

STUDYING AND LEARNING

Studying and learning go together. Learning is the outcome of studying. If there is no learning, we can infer that there is no studying. Knowledge is infinite. This is why learning never stops and student life never ends. Sri Ramakrishna said, 'as long as I live, so long do I learn.' If an enlightened being like Sri Ramakrishna said that, it should apply all the more for us who are on our journey toward light.

Nothing stays the same in this world, neither on the physical plane, nor on the plane of ideas. The phenomenal world is constantly changing. If we think we have finished learning, very soon, what we know will become outdated.

While there are enduring principles in the world, their expressions and impact on our lives change over time, and it is important for us to understand and adapt to these changes. If we want to live rather than exist, we must keep our mind alive and alert. By being receptive to new ideas, we maintain freshness and enthusiasm. We remain alert to the science of human possibilities.

While our physical capabilities will tend to diminish with age, it is possible to maintain a kind of youthfulness through our mind. This comes from studying. As physical exercise is conducive to physical health, exercise of the mind through study is conducive to a healthy and disciplined mind. Psychologically, the systematic nature of study curbs the restlessness of the mind.

Study is the systematic acquisition of information and knowledge. Study may or may not be based on books or anything written. There are some traditional forms of study (for example, in music or drama) that do not use books, and one may not even be allowed to write anything down. The Vedic tradition of teaching and learning was primarily oral. While Socrates, as conveyed by Plato, emphasized the significance of the oral method for transmitting knowledge, he also expressed reservations about the use of writing, highlighting its limitations compared to oral communication.

Study may or may not involve acquiring a lot of information. There is a difference between knowledge and information. Knowledge is meta-information, or processed information. Knowledge is information about information: relationships and patterns. Information can be compared to raw foodstuffs. Before they become useful for us, we have to clean and then cook raw foodstuffs. Similarly, with information, first, we have to clean it: that means filtering out good information from bad. It means to apply *viveka* to distinguish misinformation and incomplete information from accurate and complete information. Second, we have to cook it: that means to think about it. Then information becomes knowledge. Information comes from the senses and from observation. Knowledge comes from thinking and processing information.

One can engage in study with a teacher or without a teacher. The most difficult study is without a teacher and without a book. In this case, one has to rely extensively on observation, experimentation, trial and error, and on reflection. Because of trial and error, it is more time-consuming. All methods of study are meant to minimize the waste of time due to trial and error. When we use a book, we rely on the author to have identified the material to be mastered. But even when we have a book, we still need to engage in observation (hearing, reading, imagining), experimentation, and reflection.

PUBLIC AND PRIVATE ASPECTS OF STUDY

Study has a public and a private aspect. Schools are for public study. They help us to emphasize the systematic aspect of study. They also provide the encouragement of a community. By myself, I may be undisciplined. I may have good intentions to learn something, but I might give up after studying a little bit. If I am enrolled in a course or a program in a school, however, the presence of fellow students and the commitment I have to make to the program will force me to continue the study and overcome my lack of discipline.

However, what happens in a school is not the whole of study. Even in schools, every student has to spend time alone reflecting on the material. The amount of time that students spend on their own in thinking, reflecting, and discussing explains the difference between the ability of students to master knowledge. The same classes may be given to everyone but not everyone learns equally. The difference is due to the individual work that students do, and, further, to the varying levels of receptivity that students may have to reflect and interrogate the material under study.

INFORMATION IS NOT SUFFICIENT

Many are satisfied with information. We have already explained that information is not the same as knowledge. But for various reasons, we find people satisfied with just information. Our educational system almost imposes this on students. The volume of information thrust upon us makes it difficult to go beyond information to knowledge.

In many cases, evaluation is based on information. Partly, this is because information has become a commodity. People are willing to pay to get information. This is the basis, for example, of all loyalty programs. There is a glut of information available. The word 'google' has become a verb, like 'xerox.' Some students think that to learn about anything all one has to do is a search on the Web, or, more recently, offer a prompt, or query, to a large language model artificial intelligence system such as ChatGPT.

One of the first things to learn in information literacy, therefore, is that not all information is equally valid or useful. Analytical skills are needed to turn information into knowledge. A further stage of maturity is to turn knowledge into wisdom.

WHY DO WE NEED TO STUDY?

So far, we have addressed the first question of what we mean by study. The next question is *why* we need to study. We have already partially addressed this. Learning and study keep our mind healthy and disciplined, and amenable to rejuvenation and growth through the brain's neuroplasticity. We become mentally alert and alive and able to face the changing world we live in. Knowledge is infinite so we can never say that we have finished with learning. Sri Ramakrishna said, 'as long as I live, so long do I learn.'

We are sense bound. A large part of our knowledge comes from the senses. All spiritual aspirants acknowledge the need to transcend the senses to gain knowledge. However, between spiritual experience and a sense-bound existence lies intellectual knowledge. Learning to study properly prepares us for contemplation and meditation.

Developing the power of reason can help to prevent us from making mistakes and falling into self-delusion. Some people advocate the strangest things in the name of religion or even in the name of social well-being. Our reasoning faculty has to be strong enough that we can decide whether the arguments are sensible or not. This is called *viveka*.

The intellectual faculty exists in all of us and is active. If it is not deliberately engaged in study, it will engage itself in other things that may not be healthy. For example, we may start a meaningless analysis of people's actions and words. We might ask: "What did he really mean by that?" An untended garden tends to grow weeds. It requires work to even keep a field fallow, let alone growing crops. Before you know it, weeds spring up from where we do not know. Study is a safety net for the mind: the mind's focus can vacillate, empowered sometimes in positive and constructive patterns of thought, and, at other times, ensnared in patterns of thinking that may be negative or destructive. A habit of study gives a lower bound for the mind.

Thus, this gives us four more reasons to study:

1. Intellectual knowledge is a transition from the sensory to the spiritual.
2. Strengthening our reasoning ability prevents us from falling into self-delusion: this is relevant in spiritual life as well as in our 'ordinary' life.
3. Our intellect becomes engaged constructively rather than destructively.

4. Our intellect offers us protection from the oscillations of the mind.

Patanjali, the great teacher of *Raja Yoga*, includes *swadhyaya* as a *niyama*. *Swadhyaya* is self-study or reflection. *Niyama* is an obligatory discipline.[54] Since the other *niyamas* relate to moral and ethical values, we may assume that the study to which Patanjali refers should be such as to strengthen our moral and ethical sense.

Some think that study is not necessary for a spiritual aspirant; they contend it is enough to cultivate love for God. However, love and knowledge are not different. As Swami Sarvagatananda often said, 'what you know, you love; and what you love, you know,' a profound statement that deserves its own volume to understand.

Those who think study is not necessary in spiritual life are those who equate study with an intellectual study of scriptures, in other words, with information from the scriptures. Sri Ramakrishna told the story of the mango orchard. We should eat the mangos rather than occupying ourselves with counting how many trees there are, how many leaves there are and so on. This is of course true; however,

54 *Raja Yoga* is the yoga of mind. It is a great work on psychology and Patanjali's *sutras* on the subject (dated to around the second century BCE) bring into a systematic focus the eight steps to gradually build ourselves physically, psychologically, and spiritually to a heightened sense of awareness. Though it is in essence a work on psychology, Patanjali sets forth many preliminary and preparatory steps, and the first direct psychological discipline doesn't begin until the fifth step. The first two steps are about moral and ethical excellence and while the first tells us what we should avoid, the second step of *niyama* tells us what we should practice. It is a list of five disciplines, one of which is *swadhyaya*, or self-study and reflection.

some knowledge will actually help us to eat and enjoy and benefit from the mangos. For example, we need to know the difference between a ripe mango and an unripe mango and how we can use each kind. We need to know the difference between a healthy fruit and a diseased fruit. We need to know the impact on our digestive system of consuming one or more mangoes.

As we have already discussed, study is not just the acquisition of information, but accurate information certainly does form an important part of study. Study is not purely an intellectual exercise, but it is necessary to exercise the intellect in processing information into knowledge. And beyond the particular topic being studied, intellectual study is beneficial since it exercises the power of the intellect. Further, it nurtures us to see the power of our own contributions to push the boundaries of knowledge still further, to advance the science of our individual possibility.

In spiritual life, the source of information that many reach out to is scripture. It is also scripture that is subjected to a lot of intellectual analysis by theologians in their attempt to extract its true import. This approach does have meaning in the sense that the scriptures of all traditions record the words of the enlightened teachers of that tradition. However, all scripture has its limitations.[55]

55 This is perhaps why Sri Ramakrishna warned that *grantha* or scripture can become a rope to bind a spiritual aspirant. So, we need not overdo it. But most of us are in fact not in danger of overdoing study; rather, we are at the other extreme and are fairly ignorant of its content!

The *Mundaka Upanishad* speaks of *apara vidya*, or lower knowledge, and says that spiritual knowledge is *para vidya*. Some aspirants use that as an argument to conclude that the only thing we should study is scriptures since everything else is lower knowledge or that we need not study anything. However, the *Upanishad* includes scriptures in *apara vidya*. The meaning of *para* is supreme (not higher), in other words, complete. Then *apara* is incomplete. But that is not a reason to reject it. As we have already said, study engages the mind and curbs some restlessness. Moreover, intellectual conviction precedes experience. We have to be intellectually convinced that what we are seeking is truth. This gives us a way to withstand challenges to our faith. It is not always possible to insulate ourselves from ways of thinking that can be unsettling to our faith. If we have developed a habit of study and reflection, we will be able to withstand those challenges.

THE ART OF STUDY

The art of studying has at least eight components. They are:

- Identifying the goal of our study
- A prayerful approach to teacher and subject
- Recognizing which stage of study we are at
- Developing a habit of taking notes and rewriting those notes
- Spending time in thinking and reflecting
- Asking questions

- Engaging in fruitful discussion
- Being regular

We shall discuss each of these in detail.

IDENTIFYING THE GOAL

The goal will determine what and how we need to study. Also, note that our goal may evolve or even change with time. If we want to be sufficiently informed of current events, the daily newspaper will suffice. Perhaps we can improve the quality of information by consulting several newspapers. But if we want to become an authority on some current event, it requires deeper study. If we are trying to lead a spiritual life, studying the lives of the exemplars of the virtues we are trying to practice can be a great help. This will not help us to understand current events, nor will the newspapers help us to live a spiritual life. We have to be clear on our goal and study appropriately.

If we are not clear on our goal, study becomes more difficult. The goal can be greatly varied, and might include: to pass an exam, exercise the mind, become master of a subject, discover something new, and to find the truth. Sometimes, failure comes not because the student is not qualified, but because she has undertaken study of something that is not directly related to her goal or she is employing a method that is not suitable for that goal.

Misalignment between goal and course of study can produce disastrous results. A genius will appear to be a fool and a fool might appear to be a genius. For example, an ordinary person who happens to have already studied a certain subject is placed in a class where that very subject is being taught for the first time. Naturally, this person will shine and may even be considered a genius.

In teaching mathematics, I have often found that an important cause of success or failure is alignment or misalignment between the goal of the student and the goal of the instruction. This is why a course on calculus for students intending to study medicine needs to be very different from a course on the same subject for students whose goal is to specialize in mathematics. Once we make this alignment, we find that student success rates in the performance of calculus significantly increase.

PRAYERFUL ATTITUDE

Despite all our analyses, learning is still mysterious. It is like growing a plant. We can follow a scientific and systematic approach, but there are circumstances beyond our control and perhaps beyond our knowledge. Of ten seeds planted, perhaps one germinates.

The *Gita* says[56] that when we approach teachers with humility and reverence, they will tend to open up the secrets of their knowledge. We have to be prayerful and reverential. This attitude has been codified in the concept of a 'goddess of learning.' Knowledge is sacred and we must pray that knowledge be revealed to us and that

56 *Bhagavad Gita*, Chapter 4, Verse 34

we are able to understand it. This is the meaning of the famous and ancient *Gayatri mantra*: May that supreme and adorable light of knowledge illumine our understanding.

STAGES OF STUDY

We cannot avoid learning the alphabet before studying deeper thoughts. This level of study consists of routine repetition and memorization. At this level, it is all about information.

We may need guidance here to know how much constitutes enough information. This stage never really ends. We have to keep an open mind for new information while starting the processing of the information we already have.

The next stage consists of looking for patterns and connections in the information. This is called thinking. This is the phase when we ask questions. At the outset, not having enough questions indicates a lack of attention. At a later stage, having too many questions indicates not enough thinking. It is said that a fool can ask more questions than a sage can answer.

We have to be ready for the answer: the ground has to be prepared within us for the answer to make sense. In the *Prasna Upanishad*, some students come to ask questions. The sage asks them to practice *tapasya* for a hundred years before answering their questions. The idea is that unless the restlessness of the mind is curbed to some extent, the answers will not have any effect.

Humility and reverence will also help us to understand what stage we are at. If we have difficulty with routine aspects of the subject, we are still at the first level. It may appear routine and we may be restless to skip it and jump to the next level. However, if we can curb that restlessness and do more routine drills, we will be better prepared for the next stage.

THE HABIT OF NOTE-TAKING

In listening or in reading, taking notes is a great help in retaining information. It engages more than one sense and so increases the chances of retention because of our large dependence on the senses. A good habit is to follow-up by rewriting one's notes.

Writing has a powerful neurological coating effect on the mind; it activates the dopamine neurotransmitter function in the brain and the chemical, dopamine, gives salience and memory to the words. There is benefit in attentively and carefully copying a text in one's own hand. This was an old discipline before the printing press was invented. It is time-consuming, but it is a powerful tool in study. Copying a text can be supplemented by preparing a list of questions for oneself. One can then test oneself on mastery of the material by trying to answer the questions. If we find we have trouble with a question, we need to review that part of the material again. This exercise addresses Socrates's concern that writing will atrophy the memory. If we think that our work is complete once we have written something, we are mistaken. It is but a step, and we have to review the writing and think about the content. In that way, writing becomes a helpful tool for developing and sharpening memory.

After this process of study, the writing can be thrown away if we want. Writing is only a tool. Sri Ramakrishna says that one needs a shopping list to know what to procure at the store. Once that is known, the shopping list is useless and can be discarded. Of course, one can also maintain the notes and even improve upon them for possible use by those coming afterwards. This is usually the genesis of essays or books.

THINKING AND REFLECTING

What is thinking? According to Swami Sarvagatananda, 'coherent, conscious, correlation of ideas is called thinking.' Thinking requires raw material: we cannot think in a vacuum. That raw material comes from the senses. In humans, the traditional five senses are sight (visual), sound (auditory), touch (tactile), taste (gustatory), and smell (olfactory). Additionally, the vestibular sense is responsible for balance and spatial orientation, while the proprioceptive sense provides information about body position and movement. But to Swami Sarvagatananda, thinking would necessarily also demand drawing on dreams and imagination, too.

We have to deliberately find stable patterns and relationships between ideas. Beyond that, there is a hidden process at play. Having done what we can do, we have to let the mind go on working, and wait patiently.

The power that drives the mind is interest and desire. Our desire to know or understand something makes the mind continue to work. By itself, it discovers more and newer stable patterns. This is what gives rise to the 'eureka' moments. A eureka moment might, for example, be one that tells you your innate strengths and how best to amplify them to serve your community, in service of the science of human possibilities. But the 'eureka' moment doesn't come without all the preparation of conscious effort. It is the prepared mind that is the fit recipient for the discovery.

THE ART OF ASKING GOOD QUESTIONS

It requires preparation to ask a good question. Before we ask a question publicly, we should ask ourselves the question. If someone asks a good question, you may infer that they have spent some time in study. The benefit individuals derive from an answer is influenced by the quality of their study. Being unprepared may lead to missed opportunities, even if a good question is asked, akin to Pilate's inquiry to Christ:, 'what is the truth?'

THE IMPORTANCE OF DISCUSSION

The *Taittiriya Upanishad* says that one should both study and speak to others.[57] Discussion helps to clarify our understanding. In trying to explain concepts to others, we find the gaps in our knowledge. In

57 *Taittiriya Upanishad*, I.11.1: *swadhyaya pravacanabhyam na pramaditavyam*

listening to the explanation of others, we get some hints to further our own study. Group study and self-study are both needed to advance clarity of thought and depth of understanding. I think this is why the *Upanishad* exhorts us to not only study in private, but also to speak with others. Swami Vivekananda used to make the monks and the monks in training stand up in meetings and speak briefly about spiritual topics. This was to help them in their studies.

However, depending on one's stage, one should also be judicious about who one gets into a discussion with. Some people actually disturb our mind. We want discussion and not argument. The difference between the two is important to understand. In discussion, both sides are trying to gain understanding. In argument, each side is trying to establish that their understanding is correct and that the understanding of the other is incorrect.

We need to be watchful of whether someone is interested in engaging in discussion or in argument, or worse yet, of being plain derogative.[58] Questioning is good but it should be constructive. We want constructive guidance and encouragement, not destructive cynicism and discouragement. If we don't see a constructive attitude, then it may be better to discontinue that conversation. It is important to understand that all knowledge is based on assumptions. This

58 Swami Nikhilananda describes an incident illustrating this. Swami Vivekananda was once challenged in a public lecture by a Scotsman: 'Swami, what is the difference between a *baboo* and a *baboon*?' As Nikhilananda explains, *baboo* was used in Northern India in a way similar to the way Mr. is used in the west. The questioner was intending to be derisive. Vivekananda instantly replied, 'Oh, not much. It is like the difference between a sot and a *Scot* – just the difference of a letter' (*Vivekananda – A Biography*, by Swami Nikhilananda, p. 99).

applies to our knowledge as well as to the claims made by others. The question is how to be clear on which assumptions we are willing to accept.

I have applied these principles with my graduate students and it has been very successful. Once a week, we have a seminar in which students take turns speaking about their research. If they are at the beginning of their thesis work, the talk will be more expository about the papers they are studying. If their work is at a more advanced stage and they are developing original ideas, the talk will be a report on where their work stands. Participants are encouraged to engage in constructive questioning during seminars, fostering deep understanding and the refinement of ideas. These sessions have proven instrumental in enhancing comprehension, revealing overlooked details, and providing guidance for advancing work, even shaping doctoral theses over time. The pivotal element of these seminars' success lies in creating a safe space for open dialogue; interruption is encouraged, but only if it is constructive. Additionally, to cultivate a nurturing atmosphere, a mid-seminar break is taken for a shared, lavish lunch experience.

THE IMPORTANCE AND POWER OF REGULARITY

Swami Vivekananda's wisdom, "many a little makes a mickle," highlights the power of consistency in studying. Devoting just a few minutes daily accumulates over time, enabling the completion of substantial books by reading a few pages each day. Echoing this sentiment, motivational speaker Les Brown suggests that reading and comprehending one book per month in a chosen field can elevate one to the top five percent of global experts within five years.

Swami Vivekananda describes education as 'the nervous association of ideas.' Patterns have to be made at the level of neurons and nerves. The mind, you will recall from earlier passages of this book, is an association machine. Regularity and repetition strengthens those associations. When we try to concentrate our mind during study, reflection and meditation, we are doing the same thing but it is much more difficult.

What is actually achieved by regularity? The mind is naturally restless and resists any attempt to discipline it. This is why we find it difficult to keep up any pattern of discipline. We can all reflect on how much difficulty we have in doing anything for more than a few days. Even when the discipline has obvious benefits (such as improved health), we find it difficult to maintain it. This is because, at present, our mind is very restless and flits from one topic to another. Some deliberate effort is needed to make it rest on one topic.

It is easier to concentrate the mind when we practice regularity in other things including exercise, diet, study, and even in attitudes such as gratitude. If we normally have lunch around noon, we will tend to feel hungry around that time. If we normally go to sleep at 10 p.m., we will tend to feel sleepy around that time. Hebb's Law is in full operation, and our psycho-physical system will obey that law. What we are used to doing we will want to continue to do.

The important thing to recognize is that this also applies to our psychological state, such as our mood. Through the regular practice of gratitude, we will tend to be grateful even in advance of receiving anything. As a result, this inclines us toward a positive and receptive attitude. Establishing a consistent routine cultivates a mindset for daily meditation and study, creating a sense of discomfort when interruptions occur. This dedication extends to the realm of understanding, where regular efforts to deepen comprehension lead to the development of a natural proficiency that unlocks deeper layers of the mind, fostering the growth of intuition.

ADAPTING THESE TECHNIQUES TO SPIRITUAL LIFE

How can we adapt all of this to spiritual life? Let us begin with the goal. In the first place, not everyone is attracted to spiritual life for the same reason. The vast majority are not interested in God. What we are interested in is living a good life as decent human beings, at peace with ourselves, our surroundings and with our fellow human beings.

Spiritual life begins with life. Those who contemplated deeply about life and about the human situation realized a vast reality that transcends the phenomenal world. It is good to know about that, but we have to begin where we are.

Remember that goals are not static and they evolve. We have to think carefully about where we are and what our goal at this stage is. If our goal is to discover peace, then our spiritual study should be appropriate for that. The texts that we select for study should give us guidance in this regard. Any text that we study should elicit questions on its relevance to our goal. Mostly, this means questions about moral and ethical values.

PRAYERFUL ATTITUDE

Prayer makes us patient. Life is full of unknowns. You cannot learn everything at once. You cannot understand everything at once. Prayer is an acknowledgement of the mysterious role of time in this process of personal growth.

RECOGNIZING OUR STAGE

This qualifies what we study and for how long we study. Every spiritual tradition has writings that help us to understand our stage. Some are expressed more universally than others, but all are valuable in this process. I personally find the *Gita* and *The Gospel of Sri Ramakrishna* to contain many insights that are helpful to me.

TAKING NOTES

It is astonishing how many lectures people attend without being able afterwards to repeat a single point that they heard. Very often, the only thing that is retained is an amusing incident that the speaker might have recounted. At the same time, there is unanimous consent that the lectures were very inspiring. That inspiration will be a passing phenomenon unless we are able to retain more of what was actually said and what we personally found inspiring and why.

Contrary to Socrates's view on this particular matter, the practice of taking notes during lectures and from books, followed by reviewing and reflecting on them, significantly aids in retaining and enhancing comprehension of the material. Sometimes, something that sounds obvious when it is said does not seem so obvious when we read our own notes. That stimulates our own reflection and thinking, deepens our understanding, and helps us to assimilate the ideas.

THINKING AND REFLECTING

We need to set aside some time for thinking and reflecting. It is good to keep a notebook and write down our own thoughts. This notebook should be considered personal so one can write freely. After studying something, we should ask ourselves, 'what does this mean to me?' We have to ask not only for the meaning, but 'the meaning of the meaning' as Swami Sarvagatananda used to tell us. And this should be made into a habit so that the mind naturally gravitates toward it.

Learn the art of concentrated thinking. Vivekananda says:

> How has all the knowledge in the world been gained but by the concentration of the powers of the mind? The world is ready to give up its secrets if we only know how to knock, how to give it the necessary blow. The strength and force of the blow come through concentration. There is no limit to the power of the

> human mind. The more concentrated it is, the more power is brought to bear on one point; that is the secret.[59]

On another occasion, he said:

> The more this power of concentration, the more knowledge is acquired, because this is the one and only method of acquiring knowledge. Even the lowest shoeblack, if he gives more concentration, will black shoes better; the cook with concentration will cook a meal all the better. In making money, or worshipping God, or in doing anything, the stronger the power of concentration, the better will that thing be done. This is the one call, the one knock, which opens the gates of nature, and lets out floods of light. This, the power of concentration, is the only key to the treasure-house of knowledge.[60]

We have to understand also that what gives life and power to concentration is the desire to know. Vivekananda's own life gives many illustrations of the truth of this. In 1891, he was traveling throughout India, and, in the city of Jaipur, he met a Sanskrit grammarian. He took the opportunity to study the famous work *Ashtadhyayi* on this subject and asked the grammarian to teach it to him. This work is considered quite difficult as it is written in an aphoristic style, with each statement formulated as a *sutra* in a

59 *Complete Works*, Volume 1, pp. 130-131.
60 *Complete Works*, Volume 2, p. 391.

pithy form. The scholar agreed to teach him and started to explain the commentary on the first *sutra*, and this continued for three days. However, Vivekananda felt that he was not able to understand it, and there ensued a degree of frustration on the part of both teacher and student. Feeling a determination to correct this, he studied the commentary by himself, and within three hours, found an understanding which he then shared with the scholar. Amazed at this development, the scholar asked him how Vivekananda had been able to grasp in three hours what he had been trying to communicate to him for three days. Relating this incident later on, Vivekananda said: "If the mind is intensely eager, everything can be accomplished – even mountains can be crumbled into atoms."[61]

ASKING QUESTIONS

Only a person who thinks about the subject, concentrates, and has an eagerness to know will have serious questions to ask in respect of the topic. We might have noticed that often, in the Q&A session after a lecture, many questions that we hear are either frivolous or irrelevant. Sometimes, however, we hear a spectacular question that gets both the speaker and the audience engaged. When you hear such a question, you can be sure that the person who asked it has been thinking about the subject.

61 This incident is described in *The Life of Swami Vivekananda by his Eastern and Western Disciples*, Volume 1, pp. 277-278, Advaita Ashrama, Mayavati, 1979.

DISCUSSION

We actually have plenty of opportunity for good discussion if we seek it out. We should try to challenge ourselves to remember a few things from any lecture and compare our notes with others. In this way, the message of the lecture will be reinforced. Something that I might have missed might have been picked up by you. Also, a question that might not have occurred to me might be raised by you.

BEING REGULAR

As we have seen in this chapter, regularity of study is crucial, especially when tackling challenging subjects. By consistently studying difficult topics, mastery is achievable, leading to a sense of astonishment and confidence. This newfound confidence empowers individuals to recognize their unique perspectives, identify gaps in existing ideas, and offer insightful solutions that illuminate these gaps for the benefit of others, fostering deeper understanding and insight.

5

DEALING WITH UNCERTAINTY

INTRODUCTION

IT IS SAID that we can be certain about two things: death and taxes. Everything else is uncertain.[62] In spite of this, there is a tendency within us to seek certainty. We think that we will find reassurance, comfort, and security in certainty.

There are two extremes of people who are not troubled by uncertainty. At one extreme are the dullards. If they utter such phrases as 'what will happen, will happen,' it is because they are too indolent to make the attempt to know what will happen, much

62 Based on a talk at the Vedanta Society of Toronto on April 5, 2009. This talk was given at a time of great financial uncertainty following the economic turmoil of 2008.

less to try and affect it. Then there are people at the other extreme, namely, those people who are perfectly capable of analyzing a situation and making the effort to know the answers, but who have also placed the entire question in a broader context which gives them a perspective from which they are able to deal with uncertainty. Most of us are somewhere in between these extremes. For this majority of the human race, dealing with uncertainty is not a philosophical or speculative question, but an existential one, one intimately tied to a sense of what our purpose on this planet shall be. Nevertheless, once the question is raised, it is interesting to examine it in its different aspects. Consider four principals regarding uncertainty:

Firstly, uncertainty is an intrinsic aspect of the phenomenal world. All knowledge has ignorance as its counterpart. The more we know, the more we discover there is yet to be known. Secondly, not all instances of uncertainty disturb us or require our active intervention. Will the sun rise tomorrow? Will the current legislation in front of parliament be passed or not? Will gravitation and quantum theory be unified in our lifetime? All of these are interesting questions and even important ones, but we need not lose sleep over them. On the other hand, questions such as whether I will be able to complete my assignment on time, whether a loved one will be able to overcome a disease, or whether we will be able to make our mortgage payment this month loom larger in our mental horizon and form potential sources of anxiety and worry.

The third principle is that uncertainty is a psychological phenomenon and not a material one. It is not the case that a set of material circumstances will engender the same degree of certainty or uncertainty in all individuals. As it is a psychological issue, our efforts to deal with it have to be at the level of mind. The fourth principle is that uncertainty in the small tends to get averaged into a degree of certainty when viewed in the large. I do not know whether Dr. X will get the Nobel Prize in Physics this year, but I know with great confidence that *some* physicist will get the Nobel Prize in Physics this year.[63] An increase in scale decreases the degree of uncertainty. That is an extreme increase in scale, but you can imagine intermediate cases.

UNCERTAINTY IS INTRINSIC

The first principle asserts that uncertainty is intrinsic to all knowledge and that, in the phenomenal world, we can never eliminate it. Those who feel it can be eliminated tend to point to science. Some, therefore, hold the view that the angst that we feel as a result of uncertainty could be eliminated if we were only *more* scientific in our approach. They feel that over many centuries of accumulated knowledge, science holds the potential of giving us the power of total control of our lives and the promise of conquering all

63 Since its inception in 1901, there were six years where the Nobel Prize in Physics was not awarded—1916, 1931, 1934, 1940, 1941, and 1942. These years saw the prize reserved due to the lack of works deemed of significant importance as per the statutes of the Nobel Foundation. Thus, we may have great confidence but it is still not 100 percent certain that a prize will be awarded.

uncertainty. We shall begin by examining the nature of scientific knowledge from the point of view of certainty and uncertainty.

Let us consider the question of whether there is any uncertainty in science. The reason that science and the scientific approach have taken such a firm hold in our culture is because of the predictive ability of science. It helps us to gain a degree of certainty about our world and our lives. We want to know today what the weather will be like tomorrow so that we can plan our activities. Will it be warm or cold, will it be sunny or rainy, and so on? Or, more seriously, we want to know ahead of time if a cyclone or hurricane is about to strike, and if so, how severe it will be, so that we can take measures like evacuation and fortification to minimize losses to life and property. Science apparently helps us to discover certainty among uncertainty.

Scientific theories or models serve to generate testable predictions about natural phenomena. This predictive power is a fundamental aspect of scientific inquiry, as it allows theories to be empirically tested and validated. Famous examples of the predictive ability of scientific theories include the discovery of Neptune based on predictions from Newton's theory of gravity, and the use of the periodic table to predict the existence of previously undiscovered chemical elements. The predictive power of a scientific theory is essential for differentiating it from mere conjecture or pseudoscience, as it enables empirical testing and validation of its claims.

UNCERTAINTY IN MATHEMATICS

Among the sciences, there is a view that mathematics, a discipline in which I have taught for four decades, is the foundation or bedrock of certainty. The mathematical language is designed to be completely precise at the expense of everything else. A mathematical assertion is either true or false and the same holds for a mathematical proof. There is no room for 'maybe.' There is no room for compromise or for 'a middle ground.' Mathematics seems, therefore, to have found absolute certainty. This was the view for many centuries in the mathematical and scientific communities. I think it is probably the popular view even today. Unfortunately, it is not the case: mathematics is actually plagued with its own version of uncertainty.

Let us begin with the precision of its expression. The precision of mathematics is both its limitation and strength. That degree of precision is achieved at the expense of excluding a whole range of thought and ideas that cannot be expressed mathematically. For example, an intrinsically imprecise concept, such as a feeling, cannot be captured by a mathematical formula. We may try to model the biochemical processes that are triggered at the time that we have an emotion, and we can certainly study those processes and try to express them mathematically. But it is an open question as to whether those processes are the same as the feeling, or whether they are the effect of some other, perhaps psychological, process that is the actual cause of the feeling.

Let us ask a slightly different question. We acknowledge that there are certain concepts and ideas that cannot be expressed mathematically, but within the realm of those ideas that *can* be expressed mathematically, can we assert that we have complete certainty?

By what we said above, it would seem at first that the answer is 'yes,' that any assertion that can be expressed mathematically is either true or false, not 'maybe,' and so we enjoy complete certainty in its assertion. But in fact, the answer is 'no.' It is correct that a mathematical assertion is either 'true' or 'false' and that there is no 'maybe,' but it may not be *possible* for us to determine whether it is 'true' or 'false.'

I do not mean this in the sense that if we are faced with a mathematical assertion, we have or do not have the ability to prove it. Perhaps I cannot prove something, but you, possessed of more insight and ability, are able to prove it. When I say that it may not be possible for us to determine whether a statement is 'true' or 'false,' I do not mean this in the sense of ability. It is a mathematically demonstrable theorem that in certain formal axiomatic systems, there will be assertions that can be neither proved nor disproved within that system. If we find this unsettling, we should imagine how much more unsettling it was to the scientific, and especially, the mathematical, community when it was discovered in the 1930s. Mathematics, as our supposed bastion of certainty, once regarded as a refuge from the uncertainty that abounds in the rest of our life, contains structures with the same vulnerability to uncertainty as is manifest in other aspects of our life.

Related to this is the independence of certain statements or axioms. An example of this is the parallel postulate. It asserts that, given a straight line, and a point not on the line, there is a unique line through this point that is parallel to the original line. It turns out that this cannot be proved or disproved without further assumptions. It seems to be intuitively obvious, and yet can neither be proved nor disproved. When we look more closely at this situation, what we discover is that this assertion that we consider intuitively obvious, is so only because of a hidden assumption. We are assuming that space is flat. If space is flat, the assertion can be shown to be true. If space is not flat, the assertion can be proved to be false. But without this additional information about the space that we are working in, the assertion – which is a rigorously formulated mathematical assertion – can be neither proved nor disproved.

UNCERTAINTY IN SCIENCE

We may retreat from mathematics to science in general, and ask whether science has the ability to remove all uncertainty. But here also, we fare no better. Soon after mathematical uncertainty (or incompleteness, to be more precise) was discovered, uncertainty began to surface in other areas of science. There is the Heisenberg uncertainty principle which asserts that one cannot know both the position and velocity of an electron. The very act of our attempting to know disturbs one or the other. There is Schrödinger's model of the atom in which precise locations and trajectories of subatomic particles are replaced with clouds that represent probability distributions of location and trajectory. You may recall how in the early pictures of the atom, you see a central mass called the nucleus and you see little particles called electrons in a precise orbit around the nucleus. You might still find such pictures in elementary school textbooks. Schrodinger's work showed that the situation is quite a bit more complicated. We cannot say that there is a precise orbit. What can be asserted is that there is a probability cloud within which the electron will move. And, there is not one kind of cloud but a sequence of such clouds, each successive cloud becoming more complicated than the previous one. And more recently, there is the concept of quantum entanglement of photons, where light particles can apparently be in two places at the same time. This is a phenomenon that is the basis of recent research on teleportation.[64]

Such examples can be multiplied, but the implication is clear. We cannot naively expect science to be free of uncertainty.

EPISTEMOLOGY

In all of these examples, we observe that uncertainty comes with the introduction of the observer or the knower. The mathematical incompleteness theorem mentioned above has to do not with whether a statement is true or not, but whether we can determine its truth or falsity. The Heisenberg uncertainty principle is not about whether or not a particle is in a given position and given velocity, but whether we can know it. It is the attempt to *know* that entangles us in a web of uncertainty.

To understand this more clearly, we have to consider the question of knowledge from a philosophical point of view. In philosophy,

64 See, for example, Hu XM, Guo Y, Liu BH, *et al.*, Progress in quantum teleportation. *Nat Rev Phys*. 2023;5: 339–353. doi: 10.1038/s42254-023-00588-x.

this subject is called epistemology. It asks such questions as: "how do we know anything"? "Is there an external reality or is the universe that I perceive existent only in my mind?" "Is there such a thing as *a priori* knowledge?" Epistemology is a subject of great interest to both Eastern and Western philosophers.

Let me summarize the view of Vedantic epistemology. We are born with a fund of experience by which we categorize and classify. All knowledge is the handmaiden of classification. The attempt to understand the phenomenal world is a matter of reconciling sensory experience to our internal classification. All reasoning is based on assumptions and is therefore limited. Reasoning rests on the principle of causality or the connection between what we say is cause and what we say is effect. The phenomenal world that we know is therefore bound in time, space, and causality. This includes not only the sensory world but also the psychological world. Knowledge that is bound within the confines of time, space, and causation is necessarily incomplete and is thus bound with ignorance and, therefore, also with uncertainty. All our attempts at gaining certainty through knowledge within time, space, and causation will necessarily be unsuccessful.

This principle of uncertainty arising from our attempt to gain certainty, or the coexistence of the apparently contradictory states of certainty and uncertainty, is a fundamental concept of Vedanta. It is called *maya*. This word is familiar to many, but over millennia, it has attracted much misunderstanding. We are thankful to Swami Vivekananda, who, in four masterly essays in *Jnana Yoga*, explained it so clearly that a child could understand it. It is to be considered one of his important philosophical contributions.

So, what is *maya*? Swami Vivekananda explains it thus: "There is this contradiction in knowledge. It seems that man can know everything, if he only wants to know; but before he has gone a few steps, he finds an adamantine wall which he cannot pass. All his work is in a circle, and he cannot go beyond that circle. The problems which are nearest and dearest to him are impelling him on and calling, day and night, for a solution, but he cannot solve them, because he cannot go beyond his intellect. And yet that desire is implanted strongly in him."[65]

Understanding that the uncertainty is intrinsic gives us a method of dealing with it. We will never be in a position where uncertainty does not exist, and we are not alone in this. Everyone is subject to the same limitation. This philosophical understanding is itself a way of dealing with uncertainty.

VARIETIES OF UNCERTAINTY

Our discussion thus far implies that we cannot deal with uncertainty by making it go away. It is something that will stay with us, and therefore, we have to learn to deal with it. In attempting to deal with it, we have to recognize that not all uncertainty is the same.

There is uncertainty in every aspect of our life. Some of it does not seem to worry us. We are not sure that the sun will rise tomorrow.

65 "Maya and Illusion," in: Volume 2, p. 91.

No scientist can guarantee that the sun will rise tomorrow. However, most of us do not worry about that when we retire for the evening. We do not know for sure but we feel that the sun will rise the next day. Most of us hardly give it a second thought.

We can deal with some uncertainty, but there are other uncertainties that can keep us awake at night. Perhaps there is an event the next day that we consider important for our lives, such as a crucial meeting or interview or test. Perhaps there is some ongoing difficulty that we do not know how to resolve, such as a medical concern or a legal issue or a family or professional matter. Even after we have gone to bed, we may continue to think (or, rather, brood) about the possible outcomes, hoping for a positive outcome and worrying about how we will handle a negative one. At some point, the thought may occur that worrying about a problem will not help us to solve it, and that all we can do is to try our best. This offers us a degree of consolation, but does not eliminate the worries, the doubts, and the consequent uncertainties.

Also, if we are faced with several uncertainties at the same time, we may implicitly or explicitly order them in some manner, assign them a rank in presumed significance, and we may find that we are better at handling some of these than others.

Consider, for example, the case of lotteries. Empirical reasoning would strongly suggest that one does not win lotteries. The only one that gains from a lottery is the one who runs it. A person may enter the lottery hundreds of times and fail. And yet, the person is ready to try again. This is an instance of our deliberately embracing the uncertainty of the lottery as it offers the potential of eliminating a greater uncertainty of material want. We place such a high priority on our desire to eliminate the uncertainty of material want that we deliberately embrace another uncertainty.

As another example, suppose we have to write an exam and we are also concerned about a sick member of the family. We will tend to prioritize these concerns in some way. Perhaps the fact that we have to deal with an illness in the family might make us more philosophical in our approach to the exam. Had this other difficulty not existed, perhaps the uncertainty surrounding the exam would have overwhelmed us. No amount of advice from others to take it in perspective would have helped us. But the existence of the second problem gives us needed perspective and helps us to deal with the first problem; we prepare for the exam with equanimity. Perhaps we will tell ourselves, 'let me study as well as I can for the exam and write it and accept the consequences.'

When faced with life-threatening situations, priorities become evident. The significance of losing a loved one far outweighs the importance of failing an exam. Similarly, in matters concerning our material well-being, we often prioritize certain aspects to varying degrees.

Interpersonal relationships exemplify the diverse nature of uncertainty. Genuine communication necessitates vulnerability, as opening up to others is essential for meaningful interaction to occur. It is this openness that paves the way for profound and authentic communication to take place. Thus, we may embrace the uncertainty caused by our vulnerability for the chance that there may be some significant communication. The extent that we actually do this in practice of course depends on many factors. We should not do anything that is beyond our ability to manage.

Embracing the uncertainty of vulnerability is a key component of resolving conflict and it is not easy to do. Parties to a conflict often entrench themselves in their own position and expect the other person to cave in. Then they wonder why no progress is made even after many years of stubbornness. For progress to be made, someone has to lower their defensive shields and that requires us to say that the possibility of removing the uncertainty caused by conflict is worth embracing the uncertainty caused by accepting vulnerability. This is why Christ included such people in his sermon on the mount: 'Blessed are the peacemakers for they shall be called the children of God.' The readiness to take the risk of sacrificing oneself to bring about peace is a divine quality.

In general, we need to give some time to reflect on what our priorities are. Reflection is an important tool, and a salve, in dealing with uncertainty. If something troubles us, let us try and discover where it stands in relation to our priorities and that will help us to have perspective. Socrates said that an unexamined life is not worth living. And Aristotle spoke of how we engage in the practice of philosophy in order to discover first principles and avoid ignorance. We have to examine ourselves through reflection. That will also reveal how we came to the situation we are in, and how we formulated our priorities. How is it that we consider the outcome of a particular issue to be so important for us?

Reflection is a skill. It is not brooding. In brooding we simply emphasize our current way of thinking by replaying it again and again. In reflection, we also replay thoughts, but watch them as a witness. We try to stand apart from the play of thoughts to observe. In that process of observation, there is the possibility of discovering something new, or the possibility of altering our perspective. For instance, our imagination may lead us to magnify a minor issue into a significant source of worry. Effective reflection requires a level of detachment and a readiness to explore alternative viewpoints in order to gain clarity and perspective.

If we find detachment to be difficult, here is an exercise that we can all try. Suppose we are told that we have only six months to live. What would we do with that time? Suppose we only have one month. What would we do? This exercise will help us to identify our priorities in life (and in death). Such thought experiments can be done regularly, and it will help us to develop both detachment and the ability to reflect effectively. Swami Vivekananda used to advise the monks: 'imagine that death is at hand and work.'

CERTAINTY AS A SUBJECTIVE STATE

Next, we come to the third principle, which is the subjective nature of uncertainty. Is certainty an objective or a subjective state? Does it correspond to a particular arrangement of material circumstances or does it refer to a state of mind? If it is objective, then given the same set of external circumstances, everyone should have the same sense of certainty or uncertainty.

Consider, for example, the daily weather forecast. We hear the weather forecast for the day and thereby feel that we have reduced uncertainty about the appropriate way to dress, about whether we need to take an umbrella, and so on. But what is behind that certainty? We did not get the meteorological data, nor did we study the satellite maps. And even if we were presented with all of that data, we do not have sufficient training and experience to draw any conclusions. We rely on the weather forecast on the radio or television or the Internet. In turn, the radio, the television, and the Internet rely on the weather forecast provided by government-run services. There may be a hundred radio stations, but they all broadcast the same forecast because their source is the same. In turn, that government weather service relies on the interpretation of data provided by certain designated individuals who are considered to be experts.

In this chain, where is the objective certainty? Is it in the radio station, the government service, or in the scientists or in the satellites? It is a hierarchy of trust, but not an objective certainty. The radio station trusts the government weather service and the government trusts the experts whom it has employed to predict the weather. Indeed, the only place where there is the possibility of objective certainty is at the last stage, where the meteorologists interpret the data. There is a possibility that, given the same set of data, different meteorologists will reach the same conclusion. But a conversation with them will reveal that they are very keenly aware of the limitations of their interpretation and that there are many unknowns and hidden assumptions. As a result, there is a certain degree of 'guesswork' based on experience built into the predictions, and it is just a mere possibility that the predictions can be entirely wrong. Thus, this last stage is also based on trust, namely, that the experts trust their own experience.

Certainty is a subjective or psychological state. Once we have grasped this, the way that we try to deal with uncertainty takes a different turn. Our effort has to be not to change external circumstances, but to deal with the vicissitudes of our own mind.

AVERAGING UNCERTAINTY TO PRODUCE CERTAINTY

Finally, we come to the fourth principle that uncertainty in the small becomes averaged into a degree of certainty in the large. To understand this, let us begin by considering the toss of a coin. It will land on one of its sides, either heads or tails. In exceptional cases, it may land vertically on its rim. Suppose you are asked to predict which of these three possibilities will occur in a given toss. The answer would be that we cannot predict (unless the coin has been tampered with in some way). However, suppose we were to toss the coin ten times and ask for a prediction whether at least once the coin will land on heads. Even then, we cannot say for sure. However, we can say that the likelihood of getting at least one heads is very high. This can be made plausible in the following way. Let us assume that the possibility of the coin landing on its side is so remote that it can be eliminated from further discussion. Assuming that it is equally likely that on any given throw, we can get heads or tails, there are two possible outcomes and each may be assigned a 'probability' value of one-half. Now, if we were to toss the coin twice, there are four possible outcomes (namely (heads, heads) or (heads, tails) or (tails, heads) or (tails, tails)). Of these four outcomes, in three we have an occurrence of at least one heads. Thus, assuming each outcome to be equally likely, in two throws, the 'probability' that there will be at least one heads is three-quarters. Observe that three quarters is larger than one half. If we do this ten times, the 'probability' that there will be at least one heads is more than .999. A 'probability' value of 1 signifies complete certainty and the closer the value is to 1, the greater is the presumed degree of certainty.

Let us consider another problem. Suppose a student is taking a year-long course, beginning in September and ending in April. During the year, there will be assignments, quizzes, and midterms. At the end of the year, there will be a final exam. As the year progresses, the instructor will be able to observe the students and as the final exam approaches, will be able to predict with 'reasonable' certainty that certain students will fail and that others will pass or even do well. But, suppose we ask whether this prediction can be made in October, that is, one month into an eight-month course. Evidently, the sooner a reasonable prediction can be made, the greater the likelihood of assisting the student and altering the outcome. I explored this potential while teaching introductory calculus, a course with a large student enrollment providing valuable data spanning numerous years.

As with the coin toss, for a single student, it is not possible to make a prediction one month into the course. However, observing thousands of students who took the same course, we found a striking correlation between the mark on the first test (which is in October) and the final mark (in April). This is a statistical and empirical observation. We cannot explain why it is there, but the pattern is quite evident. And that pattern could be used to advise specific students, provided that we keep in mind that we have a statistical, and not a deterministic, indicator explaining our prediction.

This last point cannot be emphasized enough, and it is an important factor to consider in the 'science of human possibilities' that I advocate. Once the trend is pointed out, there is the possibility that behavior can be altered, and consequently the outcome can be altered. Perhaps the student changes his study habits or seeks additional tutoring. Perhaps the instructor changes the way she presents the material or follows up with students. Then it is not unreasonable to see a different outcome.

Thus, uncertainty in the small seems to get averaged out to produce a degree of certainty in the large.

This is the case even in the way we perceive the material world. When we look at a door or a table, the surface appears quite smooth. But if we were to look at the door or table at a microscopic level, we would see many undulations. From that microscopic view, our conclusion would have been that the surface is quite uneven. It is true at that level but not at a larger level. Similarly, the laws of physics are well defined at the macroscopic level, but become probabilistic statements at the quantum level.

This kind of averaging of uncertainties to produce a greater degree of certainty does have its limitations. A comprehensive exploration of this concept can be found in Nassim Nicholas Taleb's book *The Black Swan*, where he delves into the realm of randomness and unpredictability.[66] The author makes the point that for some events, repeating an experiment any number of times may

66 Nassim Taleb, *The Black Swan: The Impact of the Highly Improbable*, Random House, New York, 2007.

still be insufficient to predict significant and unexpected events. Thus, we do not mean that averaging or taking a larger perspective will remove all uncertainty. We only mean to suggest that it has the tendency to produce a greater degree of certainty in many cases.

DEALING WITH UNCERTAINTY

Now that we have reflected on the nature of uncertainty and its diverse manifestations, we can consider the problem of how to deal with it from an existential point of view. We have identified four principles:

a. Uncertainty is an intrinsic aspect of the phenomenal world.
b. There are varieties of uncertainty. Not all instances of uncertainty disturb us equally or require our active intervention.
c. Uncertainty is a psychological state.
d. Uncertainty in the small tends to become averaged into a greater degree of certainty in the large.

Thus, it is not the case that we will ever be able to eliminate uncertainty. It is therefore necessary to learn to deal with it. Moreover, in dealing with it, we need only address those instances that pose an existential problem for us. Dealing with it involves two aspects. The first is to apply principle (c), namely, that we are dealing with a psychological state. The second is to apply principle (d) and seek certainty through the perspective of a larger swathe of people.

To address our mental state, we have to satisfy ourselves that we are doing and have done everything we can to remove the uncertainty. We should not have a doubt that if we had taken this action or made that effort, we might not be mired in the current state of uncertainty. Those who exert themselves to reach their goals, to shape their life according to their dreams, will find themselves in a better position to face uncertainty. They have the satisfaction of knowing that they have done everything within their power to steer their direction. That has the potential to produce an inner calmness which is necessary for taking a wider-lens perspective and for finding resolve in commitment to labors that can harness one's unique strengths and talents.

There is the story of a bird that was resting on a ship when the ship was in harbor. While the bird was asleep, the ship left harbor and ventured into the ocean. Later, when the bird awoke and found that it was surrounded by water in an unfamiliar setting, it decided to try and fly back to land. It did not know which direction to fly in, so in turn it flew in each of the directions of North, East, West, and South. In each case, it flew as far as it could and when its wings were flailing from fatigue, it turned back and returned to the ship. Having exhausted all directions and not being able to find land, it resigned itself to its condition and decided to wait on the ship itself. Sri Ramakrishna told this story to explain the idea that surrendering oneself to a higher ideal becomes possible when one has exerted oneself in making every possible effort. He would say 'tire your wings.'

Self-exertion is a good way of dealing with worry. Anxiety and worry deplete our energy and contribute nothing to our well-being.

Given our strong connection to our physical selves, engaging the body in constructive action will tend to draw the mind in that direction as well. It is said that an idle mind is the devil's own workshop. An idle mind does not actually sit still. It tends to generate unproductive and unhelpful thoughts. Keeping the mind constructively occupied is an essential component of dealing with uncertainty.

The extent to which one has to 'tire your wings' depends on the personality of the individual. Some have a naturally calm bent of mind or disposition. If we look at the life of Rama as described in the great epic poem, *Ramayana*, by the sage Valmiki, we find that Rama had the remarkable ability to remain composed and unruffled in the face of challenges, remaining unfazed by disruptions. We know how, on the eve of his coronation, he was asked to give up the throne, give up living in the palace with his family and to go into exile for 14 years. While everyone around him was outraged, distraught, and emotional, Rama took it with great calmness and asked for blessings from the very person who was responsible for this sudden change of circumstance. The *Gita* asserts that equanimity is yoga[67] – and Rama was the embodiment of this ideal.

There is also the story of 'the will of Rama' that Sri Ramakrishna often narrated. Once there was a village in which there was a very honest and devout weaver. He would preface every statement with, 'by the will of Rama.' Everyone knew how honest he was because, in

67 *Bhagavad Gita*, Chapter 2, Verse 48: '*samatvam yoga ucyate*'

selling a piece of cloth, he would tell customers the price he had paid for the cloth, how much he charged for his labor and how much his profit would be, prefacing each of these with 'by the will of Rama.' One day, he was in the temple praying and contemplating, when some thieves came by. They had just committed a robbery and they needed someone to carry the loot. Seeing the weaver sitting alone in the temple, they grabbed him and put the bundle of loot on his head and asked him to walk with them. The police arrived and arrested everyone including the weaver. When he was produced in front of the magistrate and asked to explain what happened, he said 'by the will of Rama, I was sitting in the temple. By the will of Rama, the thieves came and made me carry their loot. By the will of Rama, I am now in front of you.' Thus, even in these circumstances, he did not lose his peace of mind or develop any anxiety, because it was all 'the will of Rama.' The magistrate was convinced of his honesty and released him, and he later told his friends, 'by the will of Rama I was released.' If we can model that kind of self-surrender, we will never be assailed by worry or anxiety or disturbed by any kind of uncertainty.

Reaching that level of self-surrender is the result of much reflection on life's experiences. We might reflect on the fact that whatever has a beginning has an ending. All of us have experienced challenging circumstances, which, at the time, may have seemed insurmountable. And yet, we overcame them. No problem lasts forever. The problems we are facing now had a beginning and they will have an ending.[68]

68 The phrase, "This too shall pass" has its origins in Persian folklore and literature. It reflects on the temporary nature of the human condition, conveying the idea that

Moreover, we might see every challenging circumstance as an opportunity rather than as an obstacle. It is said that when one door closes, another door opens and we need the presence of mind to be aware of that opening and to walk through that open door. Only by walking through the door can we see the beauty of the world as it is now, and as it can become, after we imprint our unique aspirations upon it.

Taking the stance of the witness of all the changes and all the phenomena that we see around us, we will discover a greater degree of calmness and ability to withstand uncertainty. It may seem paradoxical at first, but the same witness attitude will also lessen our elusive desire for certainty. Things come and go, or, as the *Gita* says, nature functions.[69] While everything else comes and goes, the witness is the only constant. My body is constantly changing. My mind is constantly changing. But I, as the witness of all these changes, do not change. I am always present, and so, too, should you be.

If we feel that we do not have the strength to do this, then we can instead reflect on the great spiritual giants who were able to do it and translate the concept of continuous presence amid constant change around us into their everyday life. Swami Vivekananda says,

neither the good nor the bad moments in life are permanent. The phrase seems to have originated in the writings of the medieval Persian Sufi poets. It gained further prominence through a nineteenth-century retelling of a Persian fable by the English poet Edward FitzGerald. The phrase has been attributed to King Solomon, and it was employed in a speech by Abraham Lincoln. The sentiment expressed in the phrase has resonated across cultures.

69 *Bhagavad Gita*, Chapter 5, Verse 14: *svabhavas tu pravartate*

"Stand as a rock. You are indestructible. You are the Self, the God of the Universe." By recalling such statements, gradually, conviction and strength do ensue.

Probing more deeply into the nature of 'I,' we discover that it is neither material nor psychological. It is pure consciousness and pure love. And it is not only 'I' but also 'you' and 'us.' If we fully identify with that state of pure loving consciousness, there is no question of uncertainty, but there is no question of certainty either. At the level of spirit, such distinctions among 'I,' 'you,' and 'us' do not make sense.

And this is the final answer: ultimately, the way of dealing with uncertainty is by giving up on our fixations with both certainty and uncertainty. It comes by embracing our identity with pure spirit, an identity that transcends the mind and in which the concepts of certainty and uncertainty disappear.

6

DO YOUNG PEOPLE NEED DISCIPLINE?

DISCIPLINE IS NOT a word that we generally embrace with great joy.[70] It often connotes to us a regimen of forced work that is joyless and thankless. It is often imposed on us by an external authority and we are made to feel that no matter how unpleasant it may be, it is all for our own good and we will be thankful for it in the future.

In the face of discipline and the associations the word carries, it is entirely natural that young and energetic minds will rebel and instinctively reject the premise on which it is based. Questions will be asked about the validity of an analysis presupposing that a

70 Based on a talk at the Youth Convention, Ramakrishna Mission Vijayawada, on December 17, 2004.

possibility of forced labor for a transgression will yield magnificent fruits in the future for the transgressor. 'If your analysis is wrong,' our young enquirers might point out, 'we would have lost our golden opportunity to enjoy life. Moreover, our generation likes to be natural. We don't like the idea of regimentation or being made to act like machines. We would like to be free and spontaneous.'

These are very valid concerns and cannot – indeed, should not – be dismissed without careful consideration. Let us delve into the meaning of the word 'discipline' and ask whether it is of relevance to us, and to the science of human possibilities. Is discipline just a quaint remnant of a bygone era, which improvements and advancements in the style and quality of life have made irrelevant? Or is it a tool that will help us to shape ourselves into what we want to be? This is the question that I would like to discuss in service of empowering young people, and all people.

It is reasonable to begin by being clear on what the word means. According to the dictionary, the word 'discipline' has several meanings. Firstly, it could refer to a branch of knowledge or learning. For example, within the realm of Science, there are several *disciplines* such as Chemistry, Biology, Mathematics, and Physics. Secondly, it could refer to the training that develops self-control, character, orderliness, and efficiency. One might ask what *disciplines* one should follow to master a certain skill. Thirdly, it could be the result of such training or control. For instance, we speak of Olympic athletes as being very *disciplined*. Fourthly, it could refer to a system of rules for the conduct of members in a community. A monastic community may follow the *discipline* of rising at a certain time and spending a certain amount of time in formal prayer and meditation. Or fifthly, it could refer to treatment that corrects or punishes. We may speak of having to *discipline* someone for having violated a rule or code of conduct.

Having listened to the objections to discipline raised by so many young enquirers, it is clear to me that they are interpreting the word according to the fourth and fifth meanings given above. We, on the other hand, are using the word as an English equivalent of the Sanskrit word '*tapasya.*' As such, it is the second meaning that we would like to focus on: training that develops self-control, character, orderliness, and efficiency.

It is said that the whole universe was created as a result of *tapasya*. When Brahma came into being, he wondered who he was and what his purpose was. He heard the word '*tapah*' and started practicing spiritual disciplines. Out of this *tapasya*, the entire universe is said to have emerged. And the effect of this discipline can be seen all throughout nature.

We will point out to our young friends who want to be 'natural' that nature itself is not natural! Planets are obliged to follow prescribed orbits. The physical universe is obliged to behave according to predictable laws. The morning dew is obliged to refresh the plants and the grass. The flowers are obliged to bloom according to a set pattern. From the tiny amoeba to the giant sun, all are obliged to behave according to prescribed laws. The *tapah* of Brahma is everywhere, from the wings of the butterfly to the symmetry of the snowflake.

But now, from the *tapasya* of Brahma, let us bring it down to a more common level. Our young friends will be quick to point out that all of the examples given above refer either to insentient objects or to life forms that are not human. But the human being is a sentient, intelligent being who is free. To assert that the human being is subject so strictly to law would be to do a great injustice to humanity and would be unacceptable.

To this we reply that though in principle we are in agreement with the inherent freedom of the human being, we wish to explore further where that freedom actually resides. It surely cannot refer to complete freedom in action. Society imposes a discipline on all of us and we are obliged to act within the confines of that discipline. If we are driving a car, we are obliged to follow the rules of the road. If we are in a social gathering, we are obliged to follow rules of etiquette. Otherwise, cooperation and collaboration would be impossible, and social structures could not be sustained. For the sake of working together and interacting properly with each other in society, it is necessary to exercise control and discipline in our words and actions.

As society seeks to exercise control over the actions of individuals for the sake of advancing the community, so too should individuals exercise control over their own actions for the sake of advancing themselves. Great scientists, musicians and athletes became so only through discipline. They exercised control and this enabled them to develop their abilities until they were able to summon the best from within themselves.

In these examples, we see that discipline has become self-discipline. That is, the authority that exerts control is not an external authority, but we ourselves. Moreover, it is not control for its own sake, but the exercise of control in harmony with the idea that it will help in identifying, developing, and unleashing a hidden talent or ability. Sri Ramakrishna said, '*yan sadhan, tan siddhi*' – what you discipline, that you perfect. In other words, we ourselves are the beneficiaries of the discipline that we practice.

Discipline has three components. The first is a '*lakshya*,' or the goal to be attained. The desire to attain that goal is what sustains all our further efforts. The second is '*dhriti*,' or determination. It is fueled by the memory of our '*lakshya*,' and our eagerness to reach it. The third is '*sadhana*,' or practice. This is the actual set of activities that we practice for the purpose of disciplining ourselves and reaching our goal.

All three are essential for a complete and fruitful discipline. If we have the desire to reach a goal, but no determination or practice, our desire will only remain a dream. If we are determined, but are not aware of our goal and do not make any effort at action, we will only grow in our frustration. If we act without determination or an awareness of the goal to be reached, it will be an aimless movement of the limbs. We may make efforts, but these will only serve to sap our energies.

On the other hand, when all three components are present, our progress will be steady and deliberate. It is amazing to note the kind of results that can be produced as a result of systematic effort. Sri Ramakrishna once went to a circus in which he observed a woman standing on one leg on the back of a horse while the horse was running at a fast pace. The woman was able to maintain her balance and even jump through hoops that were placed in the way. He remarked that such an amazing feat is possible only after much practice. He drew the analogy to spiritual life, and remarked that with practice, amazing results could be achieved.

It is important to be aware that in any discipline, at first, we get apparently negative results. For example, when we first begin a program of physical fitness, initially we succumb to aches and pains. This is because our system resists change. It prefers to remain in the current state of equilibrium. But discipline is a rebellion against the status quo. It is an assertion that we have the right to choose what we will be and become.

It is in order to overcome these initial reactions that we need determination. We also need to remind ourselves of our goal. It is love for the goal that will overcome all obstacles.

Youth is the best time to begin the practice of discipline as the ground is fertile and can easily be molded into any desired shape. When clay is baked and hard, it cannot be changed, but when it is soft, it is possible to put it on the potter's wheel and give it any desired shape. The young mind and body are sufficiently flexible that they can be shaped and molded into whatever shape is desired. Whatever we want to be and whatever we want to achieve, it is easier to achieve it if we begin in our youth. That is the right time for discipline.

This is not to suggest, however, that there is any time in our life when we can afford to be without discipline. Discipline is, in fact, necessary for all, regardless of age. However, in youth, there is a natural abundance of energy and a freshness that suggest that a little discipline will result in a very rich harvest. Moreover, the disciplines practiced in youth will turn out to be our saviors in old age. This is why Swami Vivekananda said, "Do in youth what will help you in old age."

But if the abundance of energy referred to above is allowed to flow unchecked, it results in a restless and rebellious mind. This is why youth is a time when rebellious attitudes tend to be so prominent. We rebel in our youth against authority and against those who try to control us, whether they are parents, teachers, or friends. We have so much energy that we confidently and repeatedly assert that we are free beings and that no one can dictate how we should live our lives.

In essence, this spirit of rebellion and assertion of freedom are correct. But as we alluded to at the beginning of this chapter, we have to find out where freedom actually lies. Rebellion can be directed at external symbols of authority. But it will be more beneficial for us to direct it against the lethargy, aimlessness, and selfishness rooted within us. If we do not achieve anything in life, it is easy to blame others but more difficult to point the finger at ourselves. And so, we must rebel: rebel against indolence and laziness. It is up to us to give our lives a shape through the practice of discipline. And if we do this, the results can be astonishing and beautiful. Rabindranath Tagore writes: "The fire restrained in the tree fashions flowers."[71]

And as regards freedom, it is correct to want to be free, natural, and spontaneous. However, such a state rarely comes without discipline. Swami Ranganathanandaji once recounted an interview with a reporter concerning the need for discipline. The reporter said that he really did not like discipline. He rather admired spontaneity and expressed how much he liked the naturalness and spontaneous nature of the music of the sitar maestro Ravi Shankar. In response,

71 From the collection of short poems "Fireflies" by Rabindranath Tagore.

Swami asked whether he had considered how much discipline – how many years of continuous practice – Ravi Shankar had undergone to bring himself to the point where he could shine as natural and spontaneous. The state that we desire is a good one, but the road to it is through discipline.

When we say, therefore, that we want to be "natural," it is also important to ask what our true nature is. To be natural does not mean to be lazy. To be natural, we have to make a very serious inquiry to find out what our true nature is. This is the whole subject with which spiritual life is concerned. The great teachers of the world have told us that we are in essence spirit – divine beings, the embodiments of loving consciousness. To be natural then means that we should live in the awareness that we are spiritual beings and that everything is the manifestation of spirit. This is what Swami Ashokananda calls 'worship of the spirit by the spirit.'[72]

72 Swami Ashokananda, "Worship of the spirit by the spirit," Vedanta Society of Northern California, 1968.

7

CULTURE, IDENTITY, AND SPIRITUAL LIFE

IN CENTRAL INDIA, near the city of Bhopal, and nestled in rock formations that are naturally sheltered from the elements, a remarkable archaeological discovery was unearthed in 1956. Though it was known as early as 1888 that there were some archaeological artifacts in the area, no serious study had been done of it, and it was assumed to be a Buddhist site. It was only in 1956 that an Indian archaeologist, Vishnu Sridhar Wakankar, uncovered the true significance of the site. His discovery established that the place was inhabited about 30,000 years ago, many millennia before the time of Buddha. The community or communities that lived here had used the rock shelters to depict scenes from their daily lives.

In looking at these drawings on rocks, one is struck by several things. Firstly, they are extremely well preserved. The pigments that these people used appear durable and the geological structure is such that there was little or no damage from the elements. Secondly, the content of the illustrated scenes contains the usual depictions of hunting and other things that are clearly connected to survival. But one also sees a scene in which there are numerous people dancing and at least one person who is playing an instrument that looks like a *khol*, a terracotta two-sided drum, or a *pakhwaj*, a barrel-shaped, two-headed drum. This scene is striking because it does not seem to convey a theme of survival, at least at the physical level. Nor does it have to do with social hierarchy. One is then led to ask what it is related to. Why was this scene drawn?

The evident answer is that human beings have an essential aspect of their existence that goes beyond physical survival. It relates to our concepts of how we regard ourselves, and our relationship with others in our community. It relates to our need to express ourselves to each other, to members of our community, and also to future generations into posterity. The dance scene is an early depiction of what we would call culture. In fact, we may even regard *all* of the rock drawings to be a part of culture.

It is very difficult to define the word "culture." However, its importance to us is something that we understand instinctively or intuitively. Perhaps it is an 'intimation of immortality' as the English Romantic poet William Wordsworth says. Perhaps it is an assertion that at some level, we transcend our physical mortality, if not as individuals, then at least as a community. Culture is an expression to ourselves, to our neighbors, and to all of existence, of our distinctiveness. It is also an expression of membership in a certain community.

Culture is often assigned an importance that borders on worship. To deviate from one's cultural identity is seen by some to be sacrilegious. Religion, in the sense of dogma, ritual, observance and sacrament, may be seen to be a part of culture. On the other hand, it is quite possible that these aspects of religion originated from the sanctity attached to culture. Swami Vivekananda says that time tends to make things holy. For example, in Vedic times, rubbing two sticks together made fire. Now, even when there are easier and more efficient methods of starting a fire, orthodox practitioners of Vedic rituals will still insist that the fire must ignite from sticks rubbed together and that any other method is sacrilegious. What is old is considered sacred. By this, Swami Vivekananda meant that traditions become sacred. And of course, traditions are a part of culture.

From 30,000 years ago, let us fast-forward to today. In many major cities of North America, there is a sizable immigrant population. In fact, it is probably not an exaggeration to say that immigrants built the prosperity that now blesses North America. Each successive generation of any immigrant group views itself less as immigrants and more as part of the mainstream population. New immigrants, and perhaps even second-generation immigrants, however, still feel keenly aware that they are different. What is the root of this feeling? It lies in culture and identity.

While it is hard for us to define culture in the abstract, we become very aware of it when there is a commingling and a clash of different cultures. It is a common problem for members of any diaspora community to deal with cultural clashes. There are two opposing forces at work. One is the desire to integrate into one's adopted society, and the other is to preserve that which for many generations has given strength and sustenance and a sense of identity. As eager as parents may be to see their children integrate into their adopted society, they may experience some anguish on two occasions. The first is when their children are unable to communicate with their grandparents. In their eagerness to be assimilated, they jettisoned fluency in their own language, and this is the result. The second is when they find their grown children choosing partners from outside of their cultural grouping. They may be shocked and distressed, but at that point, their hands will be tied.

Except in rare cases, problems such as these cannot be intelligently addressed at the moment they occur. Attention should have been paid from the very beginning to prevent such problems from arising. We speak of *viveka*, or discernment, as a spiritual qualification. However, it is a most necessary qualification for living life intelligently, for anticipating problems and acting in the present in a manner that prevents or minimizes the chance of problems appearing in the future.

We cannot, and should not, pretend to be something other than what we are. This does not mean that we are shutting the door to our own cultural evolution and growth. We are only insisting that that growth be natural and organic and holistic, not artificial or forced.

How does one draw the line that delineates the border between intelligent and practical integration into one's adopted cultural milieu, and the preservation of one's culture and identity? To some, the answer to this is obvious. Their answer is that there cannot be any integration, and, at any cost, we must maintain our tradition in the most literal and strictest interpretation. If we examine cases in which this line of thinking is adopted, we shall find that culture and religion have been identified as one and the same.

There is another extreme that says that one should integrate at any cost. This assimilationist perspective usually holds where there is the greatest separation from culture and religion. Or, perhaps more accurately, religion itself is separated into its cultural aspects and its spiritual aspects. In this perspective, the observances, the dogma, the rituals of religion are all classified as part of culture and an acknowledgement is made that while cultural traditions of the past have been a source of strength and direction, these traditions must undergo change and evolution, while spiritual principles are timeless.

Students of Vedanta might find themselves leaning toward this latter perspective as captured in the statement in the *Rk Veda* teaching, "Truth (or Being) is one, the wise speak of it in diverse ways."[73] Thus, Vedanta takes a very catholic view of spiritual traditions around the world and finds no difficulty in accepting and including different perspectives within its fold.

Adherents of traditions with more rigidly defined boundaries are perplexed by this point of view. While they will show open hostility to religious traditions different from theirs, their reactions to the harmony of religions vary from one of curiosity to that of derision. They will say that those who hold these kinds of views are not even

73 *Ekam sat vipra bahudha vadanti.*

sure of what they believe in. Their spiritual identity, the certainty of their beliefs, is demarcated for them through what they consider "*the way*" and it is embedded so deeply that it intertwines all other aspects of their identity. Thus, to challenge it or to even suggest that there may be alternatives to "the way" is to threaten something at the very foundation of their existence. It is therefore not tolerated and certainly not welcome.

In this context, the best approach may be a modified middle path as it might be the one that makes most sense in practical terms. Mahatma Gandhi said, "I do not want my house to be walled in on all sides and my windows to be stuffed. I want the cultures of all the lands to be blown about my house as freely as possible. But I refuse to be blown off my feet by any."[74] In other words, Gandhi said that he wanted to live in a country that was open to the thought of the world. The winds of world ideas should be free to flow across the nation. And yet, he did not want to live in a house that would be blown away by these winds. In other words, stand firm in your own cultural moorings, but be open to benefit from the cultural and spiritual wisdom of all traditions.

This is in fact the perspective that Sri Ramakrishna taught. He asked everyone to hold on to their spiritual ideal, but he would add, 'don't think others are wrong.' In a world that is gripped by Aristotelian logic, in particular the law of the excluded middle, Sri

74 *Young India*, June 1, 1921. The journal *Young India* was published weekly by Mahatma Gandhi during the years 1919 to 1931, and he used it to describe his concept of nonviolence and its social implications.

Ramakrishna's teaching may seem enigmatic. If my ideal is true, then other ideals must be false. The law of the excluded middle asserts that if a statement is true, its negation is false. This is why Sri Ramakrishna's student, Mahendranath Gupta (also referred to as M), was so puzzled in his first conversation with his teacher. The Master asked him whether he believed in God with form or without form. M thought to himself what the question could possibly mean. Either God has form or God doesn't have form. Both of these cannot be true. But Sri Ramakrishna's teaching asserts that the law of the excluded middle does not hold good in the spiritual plane.

In fact, it is not even clear that it holds true in the moral or ethical planes. If this law were to hold at the moral and ethical levels, then we would have an objective sense of good and evil. If something is good, then it cannot be evil, and vice versa. But we know that morality and ethics are not that simple. Most issues belong to a grey area, where it is not possible to say with certainty whether it is good or bad. Swami Sarvagatananda used to tell us that there is a spiritual logic guiding these issues in which the law of the excluded middle has to be abandoned.

The principle of being rooted and firmly established in one's own tradition, while at the same time being open to life-affirming and uplifting principles from other traditions is what will help us to live as decent human beings, at peace with ourselves and with those around us. An analogy is given of Earth orbiting the sun. While it orbits, it also orbits around itself, as if to acknowledge its own greatness. We need to have a clear sense of cultural identity, and with that clarity in hand, we will be better positioned to explore what every other culture has to offer and how we may benefit from it.

There is another side to the commingling and possible clash of cultures. How will the members of a given cultural community react to those of another culture who come into their midst? Will it be with open arms and with understanding and appreciation? Or will it be with resentment and suspicion? During his first visit to America in 1893, Swami Vivekananda hailed the country as the motherland of liberty. At the same time, he also told of an incident that occurred while he was wandering in the grounds of the Chicago exhibition. Someone shoved him from behind. Vivekananda turned to the man who pushed him and asked him why he did that. The man only stammered, 'why do you dress that way?' likely referring to his turban. Swami Vivekananda goes on to comment that this person was probably a respected person of his community, a gentleman, perhaps a father who took good care of his family. But all of these noble cultural attributes disappeared when he saw a person from outside of his circle. In another incident in Boston, Vivekananda was chased by a street mob and he was only able to avoid falling victim to violence by outrunning them.

In 1996, a highly controversial work by the late political scientist Samuel P. Huntington was published, entitled *The Clash of Civilizations and the Remaking of World Order.* Huntington put forth the theory that in the future, conflict would erupt along the lines of cultural identity, rather than along economic or ideological grounds. The relationship between civilization and culture is an interesting and complex one. I understand civilization to refer to a society that is organized around a particular culture. In this interpretation, civilization and social organization can evolve only when culture evolves, either through a refinement of its principles, or through a more widespread adherence to its standards.

We also note that when we try to identify the cultural basis of a civilization, we are referring to the dominant ideals that the culture represents to us in modernity, and not to the cultural practices of all, or even a majority, of its citizens. For example, we associate the concept of democracy with Athens, even though slavery was an essential component of Athenian society, and women had no participation in civic affairs and were expected to remain confined to their homes to bear and raise children.

In a modern context, Mahatma Gandhi believed that foreign rule over Indian society could persist only as long as the foreign culture it embodied was perceived as superior or ideal. Therefore, he strongly advocated for the understanding and practice of Indian culture. In some sense, this perspective lends support to Huntington's theory of conflict and culture since it prioritizes India's cultural identity in the measure of its power in shaping international relations

On the other hand, Swami Vivekananda, as a world teacher, saw an opportunity for human evolution in the study of culture. Commenting on the roles played by art and utility in different cultures, he said, "Have you seen their [peasants'] granaries for keeping paddy? What an art is there in them! What a variety of paintings even on their mud walls! And then, if you go and see how the lower classes live in the West, you would at once mark the difference. Their ideal is utility, ours art. The Westerner looks for utility in everything, whereas with us art is everywhere. With the Western education, those beautiful Ghatis of ours have been discarded, and enamel glasses have usurped their place in our homes! Thus, the ideal of utility has been imbibed by us to such an extent as to make it look little short of the ridiculous. Now what we need is the combination of art and utility."

The view that when cultures meet, there may in fact be an organic growth and enrichment of both seems to be endorsed by the late political scientist Edward Said. In response to Huntington's thesis, his 2001 essay is titled 'The clash of ignorance.' Contrary to Huntington's view of the static nature of culture, Said points out the interdependency and evolution of cultures. Said contends that Huntington had oversimplified and misrepresented the complexities of global politics and cultural interactions. He argues that the "clash of civilizations" theory neglects the diverse and interconnected nature of human history and the enormous potential for mutual understanding and cooperation among different cultures.

Indeed, when we see people reacting to different cultures with an inexplicable animosity and resentment, we have to understand that the problem is not culture itself, nor its attendant concept of identity, nor what some pundits call "identity politics." Rather, the issue is that these people have erected watertight boundaries around their culture that fails to acknowledge that it is enveloped within a larger human culture, and that it belongs to an even greater culture of life which is itself in continual evolution. The incident that Swami Vivekananda described is quite mild in comparison to more violent confrontations that take place all over the world even today. Now, this may help us to understand why those who move into a different cultural milieu may make such efforts to be assimilated. They change their names, their way of dress, their food habits, all in an attempt to be 'accepted' by their adopted culture.

However, this solution to the problem of cultural conflict comes with great risk. One may end up becoming a pariah in two cultures. On the one hand, it is possible that no amount of such accommodations will make one truly accepted in the new culture. On the other hand, one becomes alienated from one's own culture and this undermines the source of strength that culture represents. As Swami Vivekananda points out, "it is culture that withstands shocks."[75] Life is full of the unexpected. Being part of a culture is like being part of a large family in which members help each other to face and overcome difficulties.

Let us now look more explicitly at the whole concept of identity. From the external world, let us enter into the inner psychological world. Our sense of identity gives us a concept of ourselves, of who we are. And we need this concept at the individual level as well as at the level of the community. It is an integral part of our lives. It gives us cohesion and it gives us strength.

If we ask ourselves what our identity is in its essence, we will find that the answer is not as straightforward as we may have initially thought. Our identity is actually made up of multiple sub-identities, as it were. We may have an identity that comes to us from our profession, another identity that comes from our social position, yet another identity that comes from our role in the family, and so on. Some of these are formal identities. We adopt them in certain contexts, but have no trouble shedding them in other contexts. Our

75 "The Future of India," in: *Complete Works*, Volume 3, p. 291.

formal identities have the potential to collide and create conflict within us. Then we will be torn about which of our identities to favor. For example, there can be times when there is a conflicting demand of one who maintains both the identity of a parent and the identity of an employee. When an identity matures beyond a formal identity into something that begins to be a part of us, when its essence becomes a part of us, then it begins to contribute to our culture. At that stage, it influences our thoughts and actions and our attitudes and our reactions.

The question of identity – 'who am I?' – is familiar to students of Vedanta. It is expressed in terms of identifications that we make as individuals and which we are asked to analyze from the perspective of permanence. We are asked to try and separate who we are from what we possess, whether the possession is material or psychological. The purpose of this Vedantic inquiry into our identity is to help us realize that while we may have *assumed* various identities, it is only our spiritual identity that is permanent. By 'spiritual identity' I mean our relationship with spirit.

But let us begin with our temporal identity – or identities. While our great teachers have taught us about our spiritual identity, to many of us, this remains largely a matter of speculation and faith. By contrast, our temporal identity is something that we have already accepted as real. In discussing identity, it is therefore appropriate to begin at this point.

Our temporal identity is not something static, but rather something that grows and morphs over time. It is predicated on our concept of ourselves – a concept that is itself built on our relationships with the things and beings of the world, as well as on our own imagination. Thus, it can be further analyzed in terms of external identifications and internal identifications. These identifications, in turn, depend on our stage of cognitive development.

STAGES OF COGNITIVE DEVELOPMENT

It might be instructive to discuss how cognitive abilities develop in children. According to Jean Piaget, a Swiss developmental psychologist of the twentieth century, there are four stages of cognitive development observed in children from birth to adulthood. I learnt about these stages from Rina Chakravarti, an expert in early childhood education. The first is called the sensory-motor stage and is seen from birth to age two. In this stage, children are busy exploring the world around them using their sense organs. Children at this stage do not understand that an object that is not in view continues to exist. For example, they begin to cry if they cannot see their mother. Existence is equated first with visual perception and then with sensual perception in general.

The second stage is the preoperational stage. In this stage, the child's thinking is self-centered and egocentric. Children begin to be aware of themselves but not so aware of others as self-aware beings. The child thinks that the entire world thinks as he does. At this stage, which normally takes place during ages 2 to 7, children begin to distinguish between reality and imagination and their sense of identity blooms.

In the third stage, termed the concrete operational stage, logic starts to manifest and the child starts to be less self-centered and starts to understand the principle of conservation: quantity does not change if nothing has been added or subtracted. Thus, the child understands that physically rearranging the same number of coins does not affect the quantity. This stage is observed from age seven to age 11.

The fourth stage is from age 11 to adulthood and is termed the formal operational stage and it is in this stage that the child begins to grasp abstract concepts: logical thinking, reasoning, and planning. The child is able to think about outcomes and consequences without actually trying out a course of action. The child is also able to form a concept of how others feel relative to himself or herself. This is a kind of abstract thought.

Piaget's theory has been challenged by some who think that cognitive development proceeds in different ways in different domains (such as language or quantitative reasoning) and not in the domain-neutral manner that Piaget describes. This is a subject of current inquiry, but we can take from this that there is, at least, some process by which cognition is maturing, and, during this process, our sense of identity also matures.

Thus, we observe a progression from egocentrism toward recognizing the presence of others. This evolution involves a gradual understanding of abstract concepts like empathy and the ability to consider situations from another individual's viewpoint.

We know from our experience that children do not develop at a uniform pace. The 'collective monologue' that is characteristic of children in the first stage of development is sometimes seen in adults. We know that conflicts can often arise when people do not listen to what the other is saying. However, in a healthy cognitive development process, the ideal progression involves transitioning from an egocentric viewpoint to a more socially or community-oriented perspective.

Another aspect that evolves is our sense of existence. Existence is equated at first with sensual perception, but if this persists into adolescence, we would say that there is something wrong. With advanced cognitive development one begins to understand that there are things such as thoughts that cannot be perceived sensually but which nevertheless exist.

However, our temporal identity is not static. It changes with time. Nor is it singular, but rather a complex mosaic. Failure to recognize this, and stubborn adherence to a narrow *singular identity* can lead to disastrous consequences. Economist and philosopher Amartya Sen writes, "there is also a big conceptual confusion about people's identities, which turns multidimensional human beings into one-dimensional creatures."[76] Reducing oneself to a singular identity is, at the very least, a precursor to narrowness of world view, but at its worst, an inducement to bigoted and even violent action.

Sen considers the question of why we allow ourselves to be defined so narrowly, and as a consequence, are willing to define others equally narrowly. "To see a person exclusively in terms of only one of his or her many identities is, of course, a deeply crude intellectual move . . ., and yet, judging from its effectiveness,

76 Amartya Sen, *Identity and Violence: The Illusion of Destiny*, p. 174, Norton, New York, 2006.

the cultivated delusion of singularity is evidently easy enough to champion and promote."[77]

It is not only those who are deliberately seeking to influence social actions who resort to this kind of oversimplified view of identity. Academics approaching an unfamiliar or new subject often do the same. Thus, Sen writes, "civilizational classifiers have often pigeonholed India as a 'Hindu civilization' – a description that, among other things pays little attention to India's more than 145 million Muslims (not to mention Indian Sikhs, Jains, Christians, Parsis, and others), and also ignores the extensive interconnections among the people of the country that do not work through religion at all, but through involvements in political, social, economic, commercial, artistic, musical, or other cultural activities."[78]

IDENTITY AND IDENTIFICATION

The things that we identify with determine our identity. They also determine our character. We can identify with external entities, individuals, and with internal thoughts. These identifications are acquired consciously or unconsciously, in the present life or potentially in a previous existence. Let us discuss the knowing and unknowing aspects of identification and identity.

77 Ibid., p. 175.
78 Ibid., p. 177.

Of all the things that we identify with, the most pernicious are thoughts or rather, species of thoughts, which we hang on to. Our mind functions at different levels, and in particular, at the conscious and the subconscious levels. Identification at the conscious level is through will, and identification at the subconscious level is through imagination.

I heard a uniquely poetic and profound definition of the concept of "will" from Swami Sarvagatananda. He said that will is 'love converted into power.' One can consciously, deliberately, knowingly decide to identify with something or someone. If there is love behind that decision, it will be effective. We tend to develop affection for that which we dwell on in our mind. Understanding this, we can consciously become attached to something or someone and develop a loving relationship. This actuates will. When that relationship is connected to a goal, the will begins to operate to realize it.

On the other hand, the subconscious mind is most open to suggestion and imagination, and quickly accepts identification. A leading practitioner of this principle was French psychologist and pharmacist Emil Coué. In his work, *Self-Mastery Through Autosuggestion*, he writes, "Contrary to what is thought, it is not our will which makes us act, but our imagination (the unconscious). If we often do act as we will, it is because at the same time we think that we can. If it is not so, we do exactly the reverse of what we wish. The more a person with insomnia determines to sleep, the more excited she becomes; the more we try to remember a name which we think we have forgotten, the more it escapes us (it comes back only if, in your mind, you replace the idea 'I have forgotten,' by the idea 'it will come back'); the more we strive to prevent ourselves from laughing, the more our laughter bursts out; the more we determine to avoid an obstacle, when learning to bicycle, the more we rush upon it."

Coué continues: "We must then apply ourselves to directing our imagination which now directs us; in this way we easily arrive at becoming masters of ourselves physically and morally. How are we to arrive at this result? By the practice of conscious autosuggestion."[79]

Swami Vivekananda discusses this principle in detail in his lectures on *Raja Yoga*. Many of our identifications lie buried in the subconscious and out of view. When circumstances are ripe, they manifest. At that time, we may surprise others and even ourselves with the way we speak and act. We may say or do things that we later regret. And we wonder how we could have been so stupid and what we should do to prevent such a thing from happening in the future. But as it stands, we are slaves to our own identifications. Swami Vivekananda says that we tell people to be good without helping them to understand the means by which they can be good. The only way to gain control is to neutralize the tendencies, the *samskaras*, that make us behave that way.

This is the problem that the discipline of Raja Yoga addresses: specifically, how that control might be obtained. It is not, as we might at first think, by repressing those thought patterns. Rather, it is by sublimating them, and through becoming attached to new

79 E. Coue, *Self mastery Through Conscious Autosuggestion*, p. 60, American Library Service Publishers, New York, 1922. Reprinted by The Echo Library, 2009, Middlesex, UK.

thought patterns. A new identification or identity is created that better suits our ideal of behavior and growth. This is similar to Coué's concept of conscious autosuggestion.

Some may balk at this idea, thinking that we may be simply deluding ourselves, or even hypnotizing ourselves into thinking that our behavior or our identity has changed. In fact, this very kind of charge was leveled against Swami Vivekananda. In a talk in the United States, a member of the audience asked him if what he was speaking of was hypnotism. His answer was that it was in fact de-hypnotism that he was speaking of, as we were already hypnotized.[80]

We must, therefore, be attentive to what is being put in front of the subconscious mind. We wonder why we have certain identifications without realizing that we have actually created them. And Raja Yoga says that just as we have created identifications to which we adhere, we can create new identifications.

The subconscious mind is especially susceptible to suggestion when the conscious mind is put into a passive state. This happens, for example, when we are staring vacantly at a computer or television screen. Unfortunately, it also happens sometimes when we are listening to a lecture. I sometimes used to feel badly when I saw people dozing off in my lectures, whether on mathematics or philosophy or spirituality. Now, I feel that if the lecture I am giving is spiritually oriented, perhaps dozing off is not so bad after

80 Swami Vivekananda, *Complete Works*, Volume 5, p. 303.

all, as it places the mind in a more receptive state for suggestion. In a spiritual talk, the themes are about divinity, our spiritual nature and destiny and so on. The conscious mind may not find such themes engaging, but the subconscious mind may be more willing to embrace them. So, if you feel sleepy, then please go ahead and take a nap as I continue speaking. Only I kindly ask that you not snore!

SPIRITUAL IDENTITY

Finally, this brings us to our spiritual identity. We said earlier that our temporal identity is so much more real to us at present that we should take care to see that it is well set. Knowing our spiritual identity can actually be a great asset in this task. Before fully grasping the truth of our spiritual essence, which unveils our interconnectedness with all life forms and the world, we can cultivate an intellectual belief in this truth by studying the teachings of renowned spiritual figures. That conviction itself can be made sufficiently strong to color our culture and our identity.

8

LEAD, KINDLY LIGHT

EVERY THREAD OF our life is woven with the fabric of light. We are alive because of the sun's light.[81] We can move around and function because of this light. Plants live and synthesize their food because of the sunlight. We burn ancient sunshine in coal and oil, and we wear sunshine in cotton and wool. We drink sunshine in our orange juice, and we eat sunshine in our vegetables. Every thread of our life is, indeed, woven with the fabric of light.

There are other sources of light besides the sun, such as the moon, fire, and lamps. However, the moon's light is reflected from

81 Based on a talk at the Vedanta Society of Toronto on Sunday, October 9, 2005. An earlier version had been given at the Ramakrishna Vedanta Society of Massachusetts and the Vedanta Society of Providence on Sunday, November 15, 1998.

the sun, and fire and lamps burn fuel which derive their energy from the sun.

VARIETIES OF LIGHT

But seeing with the eyes is only one kind of vision. We can interpret vision much more broadly, and as a preliminary, we can say that anything that helps us to perceive is a kind of light. Thus, sound and touch are kinds of light. We know how those who do not have the use of their eyes can be trained to guide themselves by sound and touch. It was a century ago that Helen Keller, a deaf, blind, and mute person since she was 19 months old, learnt to hear, speak and see through touch with the help of her teacher, Anne Sullivan.

In her autobiography, she spoke of her hands as light. She saw the world with the help of her hands. Through her hands, she also discovered meaning, and meaning is a kind of light. She described the moment when she understood the meaning of the word 'water':

> The mystery of language was revealed to me. I knew then that w-a-t-e-r meant the wonderful cool something that was flowing over my hand. That living word awakened my soul, gave it light, joy, set it free![82]

82 Helen Keller, *The Story of My Life*, p. 23, Doubleday, Page and Co., New York, 1903.

Meaning is a tremendous form of light. We know how Austrian psychiatrist Viktor Frankl held on to his life and to his sanity during his time in a Nazi concentration camp by focusing on meaning. He spent the rest of his life talking and writing about the importance of meaning and even using it as a kind of therapy, which he called "logotherapy," the school of psychotherapy that emphasizes the search for meaning in life as the central human motivational force.

Intelligence is also a kind of light. When we don't know something, we say, 'I am in the dark about it.' When we find someone who is very intelligent, we say 'That person is brilliant.' When we want someone to explain something to us, we ask, 'Can you please throw some light on this subject?' Light is associated with, and is symbolic of, knowledge.

A smile is a kind of light. In his beautiful hymn[83] about Sri Ramakrishna, Swami Premeshananda writes, 'Thy delightful smile lights up even the domain beyond the mind.' Kindness and generosity are kinds of light. Through kindness and generosity, we give light to a person and also to ourselves. We are able to see inside another person and we are able to understand and communicate with them. It is said that "[i]t is only with the heart that one can see rightly; what is essential is invisible to the eye."[84]

Hope is a kind of light. When we have nothing else to hang on to, it gives us strength and direction. Faith is also a kind of light. In the Old Testament (*Isiah 50:10*), it is written:

83 *Arupa sayare lila lahari* is a hymn written in Bengali.
84 Antoine de Saint-Exupery, *Le Petit Prince*, Klett, Stuttgart, Germany: 1986.

> He who walks in darkness, to whom no light appears, let him trust in the name of Yahveh, let him rely upon his God.

The name of God, the *mantra*, is a kind of light. The Holy Mother said that by the repetition of the *mantra*, one learns how to conduct oneself.

If we analyze all of the above varieties of light (together with the associated metaphors), they can broadly be classified as those that are based on rational awareness and those that are based on feeling. In both cases, this light makes us aware of something. That is, it makes perception possible.

It is remarkable how fundamental light is, not only to our survival, but also to our culture, our language and to our thinking.

LIGHT AND PERCEPTION

We gave a preliminary definition of light as something that helps us to see. But this definition requires refinement. Suppose we stand in front of a mirror. Certainly, it helps us to see ourselves, but is it light? In fact, if we stand in front of a mirror in the dark, we will not see our reflection. Thus, the mirror by itself does not enable us to see, but acts as an instrument. This forces us to refine our definition of light.

We are used to thinking that at the ordinary level of perception, light is the key factor enabling perception. However, though we need light to see, external light is not sufficient. Otherwise, there would not be traffic accidents in daylight. Also, people who witness a crime during the daytime would not have difficulty in giving detailed descriptions of the perpetrators. It is not only light that is needed. The mind has to be present. If we are absent-minded, light will shine but we will not see. There has to be an inner light that is visible to the mind. Ideas, and the understanding they engender, is a kind of light.

LIGHT AND LIFE

Light and life are inseparable. Swami Vivekananda said:

> "We are lamps, and our burning is what we call life."[85]

We need light to live and to guide ourselves properly through life. Everyone in a hall or busy room is able to get up and leave the room without bumping into anything. But it becomes a little more difficult if the hall were in darkness. Similarly, in life we need light to navigate ourselves without bumping into things and hurting ourselves.

What gives us light? In general, we try to borrow the light from others. We try to find people who will show us the way. We are led by the opinions of others and by public opinion. We behave as we think we ought to behave. We are afraid to be isolated or alone so

85 *Complete Works*, Volume 7, p. 38.

we tend to behave in a manner calculated to show that we belong to a group. We conform to what we perceive to be the norm. When this is done on a large scale, it also reinforces the norm and 'the proper way.' We can all look into our own life and reflect on the extent to which we do this in order to 'fit in.'

Is this wrong? Should we instead rebel and become non-conformists? Even non-conformism is a kind of conformity. Some people want to prove that they are independent and non-conformists. Non-conformism itself becomes a kind of fashion. But if one deviates even a little from the currently fashionable form of non-conformism, one is isolated. Real non-conformism is to think rationally and clearly, and to act based on that thinking. Sometimes, our action will be with the mainstream, and sometimes it will not. If we cannot think in this way, then let us admit that we dress, we eat and we behave as we do because we want to belong to a group, imagining that in that group lies our safety and security.

It is not only in action, but even in thinking that we want to conform. Nationalism sometimes circumscribes the independence of thought of even brilliant scholars; when it comes to popular media narratives, the sway of nationalism can bend norms and acceptable media discourse with a striking force. To contradict that nationalistic norm, one runs the risk of being branded as 'un-patriotic.'

Then, there is the perennial debate between science and religion, the two high priests. We go to the church of one or the other. We are either 'believers' and so decry science or we are 'scientific' and therefore do not accept any religious speculation.

The security we derive from belonging to a group, however, exacts a heavy tax from us. Paraphrasing Plato, the price that we pay for silence, for not thinking for ourselves, is to be led by fools. And as the *Upanishad* says, it may very well be like the blind leading the blind.[86]

What is the foundation of this? What is behind our desire to belong to a group? Firstly, we do need guidance. It would be the height of arrogance to think that we can do everything by ourselves. Secondly, we are all interdependent. Therefore, we must take into account the views and feelings of everyone. However, neither of these means that we should follow anything without full awareness and full responsibility.

SOURCES OF LIGHT

If we must be led, then we should seek the guidance of those who have light. The first place to look is within ourselves. Our mind can guide us. If we learn to reflect, we will get light to guide ourselves. The *Bhagavad Gita* asks us to take refuge in our ability to think.[87] If we can develop a reflective and thinking capacity, we will get a lot of light from within ourselves. We will have a mind that is not carried away by fashion or by passion and which can see clearly.

Reflection is aided by the power of concentration. Swami Vivekananda says:

86 *Katha Upanishad*, Verse 1.2.5

87 *Bhagavad Gita*, Chapter 2, Verse 49: "*buddhau saranam anviccha*"

> In making money, or in worshiping God, or in doing anything, the stronger the power of concentration, the better will that thing be done. This is the one call, the one knock, which opens the gates of nature, and lets out floods of light.[88]

Swami Vivekananda says that the difference between animals and humans, or between one human being and another, is in the power of concentration. It is said that Isaac Newton could hold a thought for days until it unraveled itself and revealed new secrets, new light.

But that is not all. There is a subtler light that even the mind cannot see. And this obscured light is what illumines the mind. It cannot be seen by the mind, but it can be felt. This is the light of spirit.

The *Brhadaranyaka Upanishad* has a fascinating conversation between the sages Yajnavalkya and Janaka. The question is raised as to what serves as the light for a man when the sun and the moon have set, the fire has gone out, and speech has stopped. The answer is that spirit serves as the light.[89]

What is spirit? It is not material and it is not psychological. Again, in response to Janaka's question, 'what is the spirit?' Yajnavalkya responds, "the self-effulgent light within the heart."

88 *Complete Works*, Volume 2, p. 391.

89 *Brhadaranyaka Upanishad*, IV:3.1-7. See also Swami Satprakashananda, *Methods of Knowledge*, pp. 87–88, Vedanta Society of St. Louis, 1965.

LIGHT AS A SYMBOL OF SPIRIT

Light has been a symbol of spirit in most traditions. We say that a person who has directly experienced spiritual reality is "illumined." The ancient *Gayatri mantram* asks for our understanding to be illumined. In the Bible (*Genesis*), it is recorded that "In the beginning, God said 'Let there be light,' and there was light."

In the *Zend Avasta* of the Zoroastrians is the prayer, "I beseech thee, O wisdom, for the clear projection of light."[90] The *Rk Veda* has as its first hymn the adoration of light as fire and as the well-wisher of the community.

In the *Mundaka Upanishad*, it is stated: "The stainless, indivisible *Brahman* shines in the golden innermost sheath. It is all-pure. It is the Light of lights. It is that which they know as the inmost self."[91] The *Katha Upanishad* says: "Through its radiance, all this shines."[92] The *Isha Upanishad* states: "By the lid of the golden orb is the face of Truth hidden."[93]

Swami Vivekananda, in his hymn on creation, wrote:

> "Verily the sun is He; His the ray. Nay, the sun is He, and He is the ray."[94]

90 *Ahuna-Vaiti Gatha*, 28.1.

91 *Mundaka Upanishad*, II:2.9: "*Hiranmaye pare kosher virajam Brahma nishkalam; tacchubram jyotisham jyotis tadyadatma vido viduh*"

92 *Katha Upanishad*, II:2.15: "*Tasya bhasa sarvam idam vibhati.*" See also the *Svetasvatara Upanishad*, VI:14 and the *Mundaka Upanishad*, loc.cit.

93 *Isha Upanishad*, Verse 15: "*Hiranmayena patrena, satyasyapi hitam mukham*"

94 *Complete Works*, Volume 4, p. 497.

In the *Bhagavad Gita*, when Sanjaya sees the cosmic divine form of Krishna, he exclaims:

> If the light of a thousand suns were to blaze forth all at once in the sky, that might resemble the splendor of that exalted Being.[95]

Similarly, Christ said,

> I am the light of the world; ye are the light of the world.[96]

And in our times, Sri Ramakrishna spoke in very clear terms about the luminous nature of spiritual reality. He said:

> I had the immediate knowledge of the Light that is Mother . . . It was as if the houses, doors, temples, and all other things vanished altogether, as if there was nothing anywhere! And what I saw was the boundless infinite conscious sea of Light! However far and in whatever direction I looked, I found a continuous succession of effulgent waves coming forward, raging and storming from all sides with a great speed.[97]

95 *Bhagavad Gita*, Chapter 11, Verse 12.
96 *John* 8:12 and *Matthew* 5:14.
97 Swami Saradananda, *Sri Ramakrishna, The Great Master*, tr. Swami Jagadananda, Volume 1, p. 163, 5th edition, Sri Ramakrishna Math, Mylapore, 1978.

He also said that he had seen a luminous sea of Consciousness. It is interesting to note that when Sri Ramakrishna had that experience, he was not contemplating light. Rather, he was contemplating the form of the Divine Mother. In other instances, also, we find that his visions are associated with light. For example, when he had the vision of Sri Chaitanya, he saw him as a radiant youth.[98]

It was not only Sri Ramakrishna, but those who associated with him who had these experiences. One such incident is described by Swami Saradananda. Once, Sri Ramakrishna's nephew, Hriday, had the following unusual experience. One night, "Hriday saw the Master going towards the Panchavati. Thinking that he might require his water pot and towel, he took them and followed him. As he was going, Hriday . . . saw . . . that the Panchavati was illumined by the light coming out of [Sri Ramakrishna's] body. Taking all this to be an optical illusion, Hriday rubbed his eyes again and again, observed all the surrounding things in their natural state and looked at the Master once more. . . .[He] repeatedly saw the Master in that luminous form. Extremely amazed at it, . . . he looked at his own body and saw that he too was an effulgent being made of light. . . . He was now in ecstasy . . . and cried aloud repeatedly like one mad 'O Ramakrishna! We are not mortal beings. Why are we here? Come, let us go from country to country and set souls free from bondage!'"[99]

98 This is described in the Introduction to *The Gospel of Sri Ramakrishna*, p. 37.

99 Swami Saradananda, *Sri Ramakrishna, The Great Master*, tr. Swami Jagadananda, Volume 1, pp. 316-317, Sri Ramakrishna Math, Mylapore, 1978.

Sri Ramakrishna himself said:

> The more you advance towards God, the less you will see of His glories and grandeur.[100]

After various visions of names and forms,

> the aspirant sees only light. . . . Light without any attributes. . . . At last, he sees the indivisible light and merges into it.[101]

Swami Vivekananda said: "Take the hands away and there is light, the light exists always for us, the self-effulgent nature of the human soul."[102]

Though it is not our own experience, we can be convinced on empirical grounds that spiritual reality is connected to light. The great souls cited in these passages lived at different times and at different places and we don't have strong evidence that they were in communication with each other. This adds greater strength to their testimony.

100 *Gospel of Sri Ramakrishna*, p. 177.
101 *Gospel of Sri Ramakrishna*, p. 853 and p. 354.
102 *Complete Works*, Volume 2, p. 356.

PRINCIPLES OF SPIRITUAL LIGHT

Just as in the field of optics, we can formulate certain laws of light, similarly, from Sri Ramakrishna's words, from which we can discern four principles about spiritual light:

(a) Spiritual reality is light, but not the light that is perceived by the senses.
(b) It is the spiritual light that is manifesting as perceived light.
(c) Spiritual light is reflected in varying intensities.
(d) Spiritual disciplines make us aware of that light.

Let us elaborate on each of these claims in turn.

SPIRITUAL REALITY IS LIGHT, BUT NOT THE LIGHT THAT IS PERCEIVED BY THE SENSES

About spirit, Sri Ramkrishna said: "It is light, but not the light that we perceive, not material light."[103] What makes spiritual light different from perceived light? There are three aspects.

Firstly, spiritual light is unchanging, as opposed to perceived light which is changing. Because perceptible light is changing, it is

103 *Gospel of Sri Ramakrishna*, p. 307.

always accompanied with darkness. Sri Ramakrishna says, "He who is aware of light is also aware of darkness."[104] All that is perceived is clothed in the dualism of perceiver and perceived as well as in the pairs of opposites. The outer light waxes and wanes. But the inner light is unchanging. This is referred to in the *Gita* as *kshara* and *akshara*.

Secondly, spiritual light is self-luminous, as opposed to perceived light which derives its light from some other source. Perceived light is either reflected from another source, or, as in the case of the sun, it is generated by consuming fuel. But spiritual light is not generated, nor is it reflected. It is the nature of the Being. It therefore shines of itself: "*svayam prakasathe.*" It follows that it cannot be perceived in the usual dualistic sense of perceiver and perceived. By what light can that be known which is the source of all lights? Sri Ramakrishna gave the parable of the night watchman who surveys the entire premises with a bright light. He can see everyone and everything, but none can see his face. For that, one has to request him to turn the light onto his own face.

Thirdly, spiritual light is loving. Just as the radiance of the sun consists of heat and light, spiritual radiance consists of love and awareness. This light is not an impersonal radiance. It is loving. There is no condition on that love. Sri Ramakrishna said, "One man may read the *Bhagavata* by the light of a lamp, and another may commit a forgery by that very light; but the lamp is

104 *Gospel of Sri Ramakrishna*, p. 288.

unaffected. The sun sheds its light on the wicked as well as on the virtuous."[105]

We may ask why there is good and evil in the world. But these are our classifications. It is like asking the sun why there is darkness. The sun will not understand what you are talking about. For the sun, there is only light. Darkness is the lack of perception of light. Swami Vivekananda said, "The vibration of light is everywhere."[106]

IT IS THE SPIRITUAL LIGHT THAT IS MANIFESTING AS PERCEIVED LIGHT

Secondly, it is the same light that is manifesting as perceived light, even though it cannot be perceived by the eyes. Sri Ramakrishna said, "[God] is the sun of knowledge. One single ray of His has illumined the world with the light of knowledge. That is how we are able to see one another and acquire varied knowledge."[107]

We have already stated that all perceived light is borrowed: either by reflection or by consumption of fuel. If all perceived light is borrowed, there has to be an ultimate source. The light of spirit is 'the light of all lights': *jyotisam api tat jyoti* as the *Gita* says. Because of this, by what light can it be illumined?

105 *Gospel of Sri Ramakrishna,* p. 102.
106 *Complete Works*, Volume 2, p. 42.
107 *Gospel of Sri Ramakrishna*, p. 174.

Though it cannot be perceived, it can be felt. We can see its reflection, as it were. This is what Christ meant when He said, 'None can know the Father except through the Son.' It can be glimpsed through revelation. But all revelations are partial and pointers to the Real. That is why Sri Ramakrishna could say 'as many revelations, so many paths' – *jato mat tato pat.*

SPIRITUAL LIGHT IS REFLECTED IN VARYING INTENSITIES

Both internally and externally, light manifests in different intensities. Both the sun and the fire-fly radiate light. Both the moon and the glow-worm give light that can be seen from afar. But these are lights of different intensity. Just as external light is of different intensities, so is the light in the mind. A little light aids in perception and cognition but not to understand. More and more light gives one deeper and deeper understanding. And based on that deeper understanding, we guide ourselves.

A small amount of light in fact makes us aware of the encircling darkness. The fire-fly lights up a tiny sphere, but reveals the vastness of the darkness around it. The *Isha Upanishad* states that while ignorance puts us in darkness, a little knowledge puts us in greater darkness.

Though it is the same light that is manifesting as perceived light, it is incomparable in the sense that it is several orders of magnitude greater. Sri Ramakrishna said, "One ray of light from the Goddess of Wisdom stuns a thousand scholars."[108] Again, he said, "Getting a ray of flight from the Goddess of Learning, a man becomes so powerful that before him big scholars seem mere earthworms."[109]

Scholarship sometimes obscures our understanding rather than clarifying it. One cannot see the forest for the trees, as it were. The obvious is missed. And indeed, we see this in the lives of Christ and Sri Ramakrishna. In both instances, as children, they solved problems that even scholars could not. Through their insights, they managed to penetrate the layers of intellectual conceit that had accumulated. We also see, similarly, in the life of the Buddha, how he was able to resolve scholarly disputes with great simplicity and clarity. In Sri Ramakrishna's life, there are several incidents illustrating this phenomenon. Once, the priest of the Radhakanta temple fell while carrying the image of Krishna. One of the legs of the image was broken. Temple rituals are governed by many rules and regulations and normally, one refers to certain *sastras* for these. But in an unusual case where the written accounts do not offer any advice, scholars are consulted. Thus, a meeting of scholars was convened to determine what should be done. The scholars all said that the image should be discarded and a new one made. But being emotionally attached to the image, Mathur Babu and Rani Rasmani did not act on the advice, but instead asked Sri Ramakrishna for his thought as well. He was asked not because he was a scholar but because in general, Mathur and the Rani felt he had spiritual insight.

108 *Gospel of Sri Ramakrishna,* p. 393.
109 *Gospel of Sri Ramakrishna,* p. 466.

Sri Ramakrishna's answer surprised everyone with its non-traditional but utterly reasonable approach. He asked, 'If the son-in-law of the Rani were to slip and break his leg, would the Rani discard him and get a new one? What holds good there also holds good here. Repair the broken leg and reinstall the image." This was so obviously correct that everyone wondered why no one had thought of it before.

We find another instructive example in the life of Swami Vivekananda. At the Parliament of Religions, as others gave big speeches, he sat there quietly and observed. When he rose to speak, he did not expound big theories or doctrines. He simply told the story of the frog in the well to illustrate why people disagreed with one another:

> "I will tell you a little story. You have heard the eloquent speaker who has just finished say 'Let us cease from abusing each other,' and he was very sorry that there should be always so much variance. But I think I should tell you a story which would illustrate the cause of this variance. A frog lived in a well. It had lived there for a long time. It was born there and brought up there, and yet was a little, small frog. . . . Well, one day another frog that lived in the sea came and fell into the well. 'Where are you from?'
>
> 'I am from the sea.'
>
> 'The sea! How big is that? Is it as big as my well?' . . .
>
> 'What nonsense you speak, to compare the sea with your well!'
>
> 'Well then,' said the frog of the well, 'nothing can be bigger than my well; . . . this fellow is a liar, so turn him out.'

> That has been the difficulty all the while. I am a Hindu. I am sitting in my own little well and thinking that the whole world is my little well. The Christian sits in his little well and thinks the whole world is his well. The Mohammedan sits in his little well and thinks that is the whole world."[110]

The piercing simplicity and relevance of this story was not lost on the audience which had been subjected to hours and hours of scholarly harangue.

Mahatma Gandhi writes, "Knowledge comes spontaneously to a *bhakta*. He does not have to wade through big volumes. But he who believes that he will acquire knowledge first and cultivate *bhakti* afterwards will fail miserably in his aim. No one can acquire knowledge in that way. Such knowledge breeds, if anything, pride. But he who lovingly cultivates devotion for the Lord and constantly thinks on Him gets knowledge without any special effort to that end."[111]

Mahatma Gandhi did not just say this; he also followed it. That is why his ideas were so simple and effective that they confounded the traditional thinkers. Consider for example, his idea of the salt march. Who could have thought that 'a pinch of salt' could mobilize millions of people?

The point is that knowledge in the usual sense of the word is infinite. Therefore, it is a futile exercise to continue trying to

110 "Why we disagree" delivered on September 15, 1893, *Complete Works*, Volume 1, pp. 4-5.
111 Mahatma Gandhi, *Bhagavad Gita*, p. 216

accumulate knowledge. According to Sri Ramakrishna, even the great sages were like big ants. From a pile of sugar, when most can barely extract one grain, they perhaps got eight or ten grains. But the huge pile is more or less intact. Just imagine, if great sages are big ants, then where are we? By our own ability, we can hardly know anything.

Sri Ramakrishna told the story of the mango orchard. Some are 'leaf counters' while others enjoy the mangos. This is not to decry the pursuit of knowledge. Rather it is to focus our attention on the purpose of such a pursuit. It is not the amount of knowledge that is important, but the depth of understanding. It is therefore better to understand well a few things than to go on learning superficially many things.[112]

SPIRITUAL DISCIPLINES MAKE US AWARE OF THAT LIGHT

The fourth principle is that one can become aware of this light through spiritual disciplines. One must light the lamp of knowledge in one's heart. How? It is by the practice of prayer, contemplation, study, and by unselfish action. Be silent and watchful. Be alert and

112 This has been echoed by many thinkers. For example, in his famous work *Walden*, Thoreau remarks: "It's not what you look at that matters, it's what you see." Here, it is the depth of understanding that we are able to cultivate that determines what we are able to see.

still. Then deeper secrets are revealed to you. There is a time to think, to reason, to analyze. Then one has to follow this with a kind of silent meditation.

The inner, unchanging light is easy to meditate on and easy to focus the mind on. In his famous hymn on Sri Ramakrishna, Swami Vivekananda wrote:

> "*Jyotira jyoti ujjvala hrdi kandara, tumi tama bhanjana har*" – The light of all lights, shining in the heart, please destroy all darkness.

This kind of prayer is answered. As Christ said, "Ask and it shall be given to you. Knock and it shall be opened. Seek and ye shall find." He also said that if you ask God for bread, he will not give you a stone.[113] And Sri Ramakrishna said that if you take one step toward God, then God takes many steps toward you. In effect, what you are seeking is also seeking you. Swami Vivekananda adds, "Light comes gently, slowly, but surely it comes."[114] He also said emphatically, "Light must come."[115]

This is not something that happens in a day. One should not be discouraged or lose faith. Sri Ramakrishna said that one cannot see stars in the sky during the daytime and yet they are there. For there is a distraction that is obscuring our ability to see the stars. Astronomers

113 *Matthew* 7:7 and 7:9-11
114 *Complete Works*, Volume 2, p. 403.
115 *Complete Works*, Volume 4, p. 127.

say that in the year 1250, a supernova took place in a galaxy not very far from us. They came to this conclusion by analyzing light energy that is measurable today. A supernova is a catastrophic event and if the galaxy is not far from us (in astronomical terms), then it should have been an extraordinarily bright phenomenon, and yet, the astronomical records of that era do not speak of it. This has suggested that perhaps this nova was invisible, in the sense that its radiation was mainly in the form of X-rays. This exemplifies how a significant event may be unfolding right before us, yet without the perception to witness it in progress, it remains unseen. We have to be capable of registering that light which is before us. We have to be tuned to that light. At this very spot, all radio channels are audible. But we need the right instrument – namely, a radio – and it has to be correctly tuned.

We started our discussion in this chapter by saying that we tend to seek guidance. Who will guide us? Firstly, we should consult the teachings of illumined souls. Secondly, we should look within ourselves to contemplate their words and to discover the light for ourselves. There has to be a retreat within to discover the underlying unity. We cannot do that without contemplation. Contemplation is the backbone of our spiritual life.

For this contemplation, we need not go anywhere special. Sri Ramakrishna said, '*mane, vane, kone*' – it can be done in the mind, in the forest, or in the corner of a room. It is not where we are, but where our mind is. Sri Ramakrishna compares contemplation with the making of butter. First, one has to boil milk and then let it sit undisturbed so that it can set into curd. Then one churns the curd and extracts the butter. If the milk were poured into water, the two would mix and we would not be able to extract one from the other. But if the butter is set in water, it will not mix but float. Contemplation makes us integrated and wholesome so that the disintegrating influences of the world do not blow us around like a leaf in a gale.

What do we discover when we contemplate? We discover that there is an inner light, the light of Being, which has been guiding us, and which is guiding us. In the *Bhagavad Gita*, Sri Krishna gives the following assurance: "For those who are struggling and who are attracted to the goal, I destroy the darkness born of ignorance by the shining lamp of wisdom."[116]

How and when the inner light is revealed is a mystery. Sri Ramakrishna says: "Suppose a man is in a dark room. He goes on rubbing a match against a match-box and all of a sudden, light comes. Likewise, if God gives us this flash of divine light, all our doubts are destroyed."[117] He also said, "When a light is brought into a room, it is lighted all at once, not gradually."[118]

Such disciplines become fruitful when they are undertaken with interest and attention. First, we must want the light. Second, we must direct our mind toward the light. This is what Christ meant when he said, 'Ask and it shall be given to you. Knock and it shall be opened. Seek and ye shall find."[119]

116 *Bhagavad Gita*, Chapter 10, Verse 11: "*Tesam eva 'nukampapartham, aham ajnanajam tamah, nasayamy atmabhavastho, jnanadipena bhasvata!*"

117 *Gospel of Sri Ramakrishna*, p. 734.

118 *Gospel of Sri Ramakrishna*, p. 183.

119 *Matthew* 7:7

Notice that we need both interest and attention. Interest is not sufficient. In the *Kena Upanishad*, a student who was interested rises and asks the teacher, 'Sir, please teach us the *Upanishad*.' But he did this *after* the sage had gone through an extensive discourse. This meant that the student was not listening. He was interested but not paying attention.

Similarly, it is not sufficient to pay attention but have no interest. Many students try to memorize information so that they can satisfy the formal requirements of a program. However, as they have not cultivated a real interest in the subject, their understanding is not deep and there is a tendency to forget the material once the pressure to remember it is removed. We need both interest and attention. Interest leads us to the water, while attention enables us to drink from it. When combined, these two aspects allow us to be rejuvenated by the water. Interest and attention mature into commitment and action.

It is said that lamps have to be kept clean and ready. Otherwise, even though the wick is good, there is plenty of oil, and the lamp is lit, the light will not come through. In us, the light of spirit is always lit. By directing our interest and attention to it, we will discover it and make it possible for the light to come through.

This process of discovery is usually gradual, though it may be sudden. We are all struggling to discover that light. We make mistakes: it doesn't take an Einstein or a Plato to tell us our mistakes. But interest and attention, arisen to commitment and action, keep us moving toward the goal. Moreover, every effort that we make in this direction brings the goal closer to us. From this point of view, we even understand that the so-called 'mistakes' were actually stepping stones along the path to success. Sri Ramakrishna said, 'If you take one step towards God, He takes ten steps towards you.'

LEAD, KINDLY LIGHT

There is a beautiful hymn by John Henry Newman written in 1833. He was a young minister in England and during the summer of 1833 he was traveling on a ship in the Mediterranean Sea. For one week, this ship was stranded between Corsica and Sardinia, unable to move because of dense fog. There, pondering his past and his future, he penned the following hymn:

> Lead, kindly light amid the encircling gloom; Lead thou me on
> The night is dark, and I am far from home; Lead thou me on
> Keep thou my feet, I do not ask to see the distant scene; one step enough for me.
> I was not even thus, nor prayed that Thou shouldst lead me on
> I loved to choose and see my path, but now Lead thou me on
> I loved the garish day, and spite of fears, pride ruled my will;
> Remember not past years.
> So long Thy power hath blest me, sure it still will lead me on
> Over moor and fen, over crag and torrent till the night is gone
> And with the morn those angel faces smile
> Which I have loved long since, and lost a while.

This poem represents the spiritual struggle. We start with enthusiasm. But the way is long. It challenges some of our cherished views and assumptions. It challenges the way we live. Many are disappointed and many become frustrated and give up.

Mahatma Gandhi is a good example of how not to give up. This hymn was a favorite one of his. He was not born a saint or a mahatma. He did not seem to have any special gifts. But he had a love for truth. And through that, he was able to struggle and lift himself up to the point that even though he was engaged in one of the most important political and social struggles of the millennium, he considered himself a devotee and others considered him a saint.

The point is that *when* one will get the light is a mystery. We do not know. While waiting, perhaps our enthusiasm dims and we may even grow skeptical. We may also have a kind of conceit that we don't need any spiritual guidance. We may think that we are very rational people and very qualified in terms of our physical and intellectual abilities. But consider the process of life. We are born as children, helpless and dependent on others to even keep us alive. In youth, we rebel and try to assert our independence. But in old age, once again we are helpless and dependent on others. If we think over this whole process, it should make us humble in the true sense of the word. It is not a kind of humility that makes us think we are incapable. Rather this humility gives us faith in ourselves but also makes us prayerful and contemplative. And then we pray, "Lead, kindly light." I am ready to follow.

All of us need guidance. All of us need light. Ultimately, we need to discover that we are of the same nature as the Light from which we seek guidance. Then we truly understand who we are and the enormity of what we are capable of accomplishing. The human possibilities within us come clearly into focus.

9

TRADITION AND INNOVATION IN SPIRITUAL LIFE

LIFE IS FRAUGHT with uncertainties, ranging from the trivial to the life-threatening.[120] We all deal with this fact of life in different ways, but we also deal with it as a society. One of the ways that human society deals with this is through customs, rituals, and observances.

The human mind seeks certainty, stability, and permanence in every aspect, both individually and collectively. For collective stability, we may agree to follow certain ways of doing things. For the sake of unity, we may agree to hold certain beliefs and propagate those beliefs to our children.

120 Based on a talk at the Vedanta Society of Toronto on May 2, 2010.

The dictionary meaning of the word "tradition" is "the handing down orally of stories, beliefs, customs etc. from generation to generation" and "a long-established custom or practice that has the effect of an unwritten law." What begins as a custom, ritual, or an observance becomes, over course of time, a tradition.

But there is another meaning of the word which is more ancient and that is not as well-known. In Latin, the root is *traditio* which means 'a surrender, or a delivery.' In other words, it refers to the handing over of something and the relinquishment of one's ownership or control. It may be surprising, at first, to learn that the word *treason* is derived from the same root as *tradition.* But here the delivery or surrender has the added connotation of betrayal. On its own, the ancient meaning of the word *tradition* seems to be the giving up and handing over of something.

From this point of view, what is it that we are giving up and handing over? It is apparently the freedom of choice in certain matters. In return for membership in a certain community or tradition, we give up our freedom of choice in terms of certain beliefs, customs, and practices.

According to the dictionary, tradition among Jews refers to "the unwritten religious code and doctrine regarded as handed down from Moses."[121] For Christians, it refers to "the unwritten teachings regarded as handed down from Jesus and the Apostles" and among

121 I am told that among scholars of Judaism, there is ongoing debate about the relative value of unwritten oral tradition compared to the written text of the Torah. It is reasonable to assume that similar debates exist in other religions as well.

Muslims, it indicates "the sayings and acts attributed to Mohammed, not in the Koran but orally transmitted." These are examples of religious traditions, but there are also many non-religious traditions.

Tradition is not arbitrary, nor does it enter all of a sudden. It is formulated over a period of time and that is both its strength and its weakness. Its strength is that for something to become a tradition, it had to have stood the test of time. Its weakness is that time tends to dilute, and thus whatever vision or idealism motivated the original custom may become completely forgotten and invisible by the time the custom becomes a tradition.

One may speculate whether a custom that is vital to survival becomes sacrosanct and acquires a religious overtone. Perhaps many of the religious customs of the world are of this nature. They come into being largely for historical reasons and not spiritual ones. In the course of time, that history itself becomes a part of the religious tradition, and the customs acquire the status of religious injunctions.

Through custom, we may define ourselves as a community. This is especially true with religious communities: some of them dress in a certain way, eat in a certain way, build their houses in a certain way, and name themselves in a certain way etc. to preserve their identity. In Orthodox Jewish communities, men commonly wear skullcaps or hats. During synagogue services, it is customary for them to don prayer shawls and cover their heads with *kippot*.

In return for membership in that community, individuals surrender their choice in these matters. If anyone in the community challenges those traditions egregiously, they risk being ostracized, expelled, and perhaps even excommunicated. The community feels that that individual's exercise of choice threatens the very existence of the community. In other words, the community is identified and defined by its traditions.

Tradition gives us collective memory and social cohesion. It may be that through acting out the customs born of tradition, we remember certain great and inspiring individuals. Perhaps these are the individuals whose innovations have now become our customs and traditions. They are the prophets and the pathfinders and they continue to live through the tradition.

On the other hand, to innovate is to "renew or alter, to introduce new methods, devices, etc." *Innovation* as a noun refers to "something newly introduced; a new method, custom, device, etc.; a change in the way of doing things."

It is not the case that every change in the way of doing things can be called an innovation, just as not all customs can be called traditions. For example, suppose we try to start walking backwards. Is that an innovation? What problem does it solve? What need does it fulfill? When people feel that they are benefiting in some way by doing as others do, they will start to follow, even if they are mistaken about the benefit conferred. For example, we see among some young people that their hair is dyed an unnatural color. This act is considered by them to be an innovation because it satisfies their need to do something different, or to act upon their impulse to be a non-conformer.

Thus, tradition is to give up or surrender freedom in return for membership in a community. Innovation is to introduce a new way of doing things. From this, we see that tradition and innovation are opposites. But in any healthy living system, both are necessary.

Sameness or complete equality leads to death. This is because the environment is constantly changing, and unless the system is able to adapt itself to the changes, it will not be able to survive. On the other hand, if the system changes too rapidly, that also makes it vulnerable and fragile.

In human society, tradition contains our collective memory and our core values that ensure continuity. On the other hand, innovation produces the variations that will ensure our survival in a changing environment. The two exist in creative tension. At some times, tradition gains the upper hand, and society becomes more conservative. It becomes very difficult to suggest anything new. At other times, innovation gains the upper hand, and society undergoes a kind of revolution. To be 'different' becomes the new tradition.

Society is of course not homogeneous and so there may be these movements of tradition and innovation happening at different speeds and in different aspects in some cross-section of society. For example, change among young people may be different from those among senior citizens. The divisions may be along multiple lines.

Traditions belong to communities and communities may overlap and may be layered. We belong to various communities. For example, we belong to the community we live in. Perhaps we are professionals. Perhaps we are parents and in that case, we may belong to a school community where our children study. We may belong to a political party or a religious community. We may be citizens of, or identify with, a certain country. More generally, we are human beings and identify with our humanity. Even more generally, we are living beings and identify ourselves as a part of the living world.

This overlap may result in a conflict. We may belong to overlapping communities that have conflicting traditions (for example, a parent and a professional). As professionals, we may have to commit many hours to work in the office, and as parents, we may want to commit many hours to be spent with our children. It may be that there are not enough hours in a day to fulfill both commitments. It is this conflict between traditions that can stimulate innovation because it forces people to question. We try to harmonize our membership in two communities and the result is innovation. In the case of the parent and the professional with competing demands, perhaps they are able to arrange a flexible office schedule so that they can spend more time at home.

Tradition does not exempt us from thinking, but often we do lapse into complacency. The conflict of traditions wakes us up and forces us to think. We are forced to ask: 'what is the meaning of this custom or ritual? Why do we follow this? What benefits are we getting from it?'

Consider, for example, the issues faced by the Indian diaspora. We see numerous instances of confused children and even more confused parents. I am sure this is not unique to the Indian diaspora, but I have had the chance to observe it first-hand in that context. The questions that the children are asking have not even occurred to the parents. Far from knowing the answers, parents often find the questions posed by their children to be unfamiliar and profound. This stems from a tendency to engage in traditions without questioning their significance. It is through questioning that we can discern the core elements that require preservation and those aspects where change can be embraced.

We have to be careful that in raising these questions, we are not fooling ourselves. The first question we can ask ourselves is what our motive is. Is it to find answers to questions? In that case, it has a positive foundation. There is a way to ask questions. Sincere questioning tends to be respectful and reverential. On the other hand, is our motive to rebel? That is a negative foundation and will lead to difficulties. If we cut the ground from under ourselves, where will we stand? This is why so many young people end up confused and feeling isolated culturally. They reject what they have and do not have the positive foundation to acquire anything new.

Some may feel that this kind of inquiry is beyond them and that it is a kind of intellectual pursuit. It is nothing of the kind. It is about the fundamentals of life. It is within the reach of everyone because it concerns everyone.

These two forces of tradition and innovation are being manipulated by all of us to different degrees. This makes for a fascinating study from many points of view. We shall discuss them in the context of spiritual life.

At the outset, let us recall what Swami Vivekananda says. He defines the goal of all spiritual evolution as freedom. "All religions and all methods of work and worship lead us to one and the same goal. I have already tried to point out that goal. It is freedom as I understand it. Everything that we perceive around us is struggling toward freedom, from the atom to the man, from the insentient, lifeless particle of matter to the highest existence on earth, the human soul. The whole universe is in fact the result of this struggle for freedom. In all combinations every particle is trying to go on its own way, to fly from the other particles; but the others are holding it in check. Our earth is trying to fly away from the sun, and the moon from the earth. Everything has a tendency to infinite dispersion. All that we see in the universe has for its basis this one struggle toward freedom; it is under the impulse of this tendency that the saint prays and the robber robs."[122]

It therefore follows that no tradition can lead us to our spiritual goal. It may point the way and even take us a considerable distance. However, by definition, tradition represents a usurping of freedom. This is why Swami Vivekananda says that it is good to be born in a church, but not to die there.[123] To be born in a church means to have the protection, the nurturing and the encouragement of a tradition that is necessary at early stages of growth.

Tradition can protect us. Sri Ramakrishna says, "When a tree is young, it should be fenced all around; otherwise it may be destroyed by cattle."[124] This is perhaps why the *Bhagavad Gita* says that one who ignores or rejects the scriptures and proceeds according to their own wishes does not succeed in achieving either perfection, or happiness or the supreme goal.[125]

Like all walls, tradition has a dual aspect: it prevents things from coming in, but also prevents us from going out. Eventually the

122 *Complete Works*, Volume 1, p. 108.

123 "It is very good to be born in a church, but it is very bad to die in a church. It is very good to be born within the limits of certain forms that help the little plant of spirituality, but if a man dies within the bounds of these forms, it shows that he has not grown, that there has been no development of the soul" (*Complete Works*, Volume 2, pp. 39-40).

124 *Gospel of Sri Ramakrishna*, p. 81.

125 *Bhagavad Gita*, Chapter 16, Verse 23: "*Yah sastra vidhim utstrjya vartate kama karatah na sa siddhim avapnoti na sukham na param gatim.*"

fencing has to be removed: otherwise it will stunt the growth of the plant. This is why we find that those who move forward in spiritual life tend to speak in non-traditional terms.

Extending oneself beyond tradition is not a rejection but a fulfillment. This is the language that Christ used when He spoke in non-traditional terms. 'I come not to destroy but to fulfill.' In our times, we find Swami Vivekananda speaking in very non-traditional terms. For example, he said that one is closer to heaven through football than through the *Gita*. This is not a rejection or undermining of the *Gita*, but rather an assertion that we have to make ourselves fit to understand the teachings of Sri Krishna by first making ourselves a little strong in body and mind.

Looking at things in a very traditional way sometimes blinds us to the potential in front of us. Among those who came to see Sri Ramakrishna, how many could understand what he actually represented? Many saw him in a very traditional way. They thought that he was a holy man like many other holy personalities. They thought that he was repeating what was already known and existing in the scriptures. These people could not understand what Swami Vivekananda meant when he said that Sri Ramakrishna is the '*avatara varista*,' or the greatest of the incarnations. They thought that he was exaggerating because of the loving relationship between student and teacher.

Indeed, a careful study of Sri Ramakrishna's life and teachings shows how non-traditional he was. At the same time, he respected all traditions and was careful not to disturb the faith of anyone. Let us consider a few examples of this.

We have already considered the incident of the priest of the Radhakanta temple who was once carrying the image of Krishna when he slipped and fell. The image also fell and broke. According to tradition, one cannot worship a damaged image. On the other hand, there was great sentimentality associated with the image as it had been worshipped until then, and the devout felt that it was a tangible representation of Krishna himself. The question was put to scholars as to how to resolve this dilemma. The scholars said that the traditional texts were quite clear on this point and that in no way could a damaged *pratima* (sculpture or likeness) be worshipped. It had therefore to be consigned to the Ganga and a new image made. However, when Sri Ramakrishna was consulted by Rani Rasmani, he said: 'suppose the Rani's son-in-law [Mathur Babu] were to break his leg. Would she drown him in the Ganga and get a new son-in-law or would she get him medical treatment to fix the broken leg. The same should be done in this case: the image should be repaired and reinstalled. God is our very own and part of our family.' After he said this, this solution seemed obvious and appealed to everyone including the scholars.

Another instance is connected to a pilgrimage to Vaidyanath. Sri Ramakrishna was part of a group that was making a pilgrimage to the Vaidyanath temple in Deogarh. The entire trip had been organized by Mathur Babu and there were a large number of people in the group. During the course of the trip, the group halted at a village where there were many poor people. Seeing their condition, Sri Ramakrishna empathized with them and asked Mathur to give them all some clothes, oil, and food. Mathur had planned the expedition carefully and felt that doing what Sri Ramakrishna was asking for would introduce a new and very large financial burden that was not practicable to undertake. He tried to explain this to

Sri Ramakrishna but could not get him to agree. Sri Ramakrishna said that Mathur could continue to the temple on his own but that he, Sri Ramakrishna, would stay with the poor villagers. Hearing this, Mathur had no choice but to fulfill his request.

It is well-known that Sri Ramakrishna worshipped the Divine Mother in his own style. The attitude of most priests is that certain ritualistic worship has to be done in order to please the deity, and that if these are not done, the deity will be angry and unpleasant things might happen. Sri Ramakrishna's case was completely different. When he worshipped, the main question in his mind was whether the Divine Mother was really present, and, if so, why he was not able to see Her. He became very impatient to answer these questions and spent most of his time, even during worship, in meditation and prayer. After he directly experienced the presence of the Mother and in such an intense way that he could feel Her presence at all times, his worship became transformed. He would see Her presence everywhere: in the image, in the articles of worship and even in a cat that wandered into the temple. Once, he fed the cat with food that was to be offered to the Mother. This outraged the other priests since they saw it as a flagrant violation of traditional rules governing worship. It is important to note that Sri Ramakrishna was not trying to violate the tradition nor was he trying to teach anyone anything or make any point. He was reacting to his own direct experience.

When Tota Puri was trying to teach him the non-dualistic form of meditation, Sri Ramakrishna was 'stuck' at the vision of the Divine Mother. Tota Puri asked him to mentally cut the image in two and Sri Ramakrishna was able to do it. From this, we can imagine how non-traditional he was.

At the same time, when Sri Ramakrishna observed a tradition, he did so completely: When he wanted to experience God through the Sufi perspective, he did not visit the temple and in fact, he lived outside a masjid and changed his clothes and eating habits to be in tune with the tradition of the Sufis. When he wanted to practice the attitude of Hanuman, he wore his cloth differently and his mannerisms also changed. It is said that there was a physical change and even a transformation of his backbone to resemble that of the beginning of a tail! This shows the extent to which he immersed himself in the tradition he wanted to experience.

It was not only in his life, but also in his teachings that Sri Ramakrishna was very non-traditional. For example, the *Upanishads* speak of the spirit as being beyond mind and speech. Sri Ramakrishna said, 'the pure mind and the pure spirit are one.' Traditional teachings say that we have to give up the ego. Sri Ramakrishna said, 'you can never give up the ego, so ripen it.' The *Vaishnava* scriptures speak of compassion to living beings as an injunction to devotees but Sri Ramakrishna said that it was arrogance to think we could show compassion to anything; rather, it was the 'worship of God in man.' In pointing these out, I do not mean to suggest that we should have a new sect of Sri Ramakrishna which is set apart from others through these differences. Rather I want to draw attention to the fact that Sri Ramakrishna presented things in a very non-traditional way.

Swami Vivekananda was perhaps one of the first and one of the few who understood the significance of what Sri Ramakrishna taught and represented. Once Swami Vivekananda told some friends that he could write an entire volume on each of Sri Ramakrishna's teachings. Haramohan Mitra replied that he did not see so much depth in the Master's teachings. Swami Vivekananda told him that he would see it if he had the brains!

Yet, when Swami Vivekananda was in the West, he spoke mostly about the principles of Vedanta rather than about the personality of Sri Ramakrishna. This led some in India to fault him for not preaching about Sri Ramakrishna, and some actually thought that he was violating the traditional relationship between teacher and student and trying to propagate his own name.

However, Swami Vivekananda was not diminishing the importance of his teacher, but rather elevating it. He realized that what Sri Ramakrishna taught had to do not just with Hinduism but with spirituality in general. By prematurely invoking the personality of Sri Ramakrishna he would compromise the channel of communication that he had established based on the universal spiritual principles represented by Sri Ramakrishna's teachings.

He also saw that the teaching had to be delivered differently in India and outside India. In India the problem was that religion was being used to justify laziness and ignoring social conditions. In the West, social conditions were being used to argue for the irrelevance of religion. I hasten to add that this kind of classification is not as relevant today as it was a century ago.

Swami Vivekananda's idea to translate Sri Ramakrishna's concept of 'the worship of God in man' into a foundation principle of a monastic order was brilliant and highly non-traditional. His own brother disciples could not understand it at first. When two of Swami Vivekananda's disciples, Swami Nischayananda and Swami Kalyanananda, established a hospital in Hardhwar and took care of the sick monks and pilgrims, they were addressed by other monks in a derogatory manner as 'sweeper monks.' And yet, today, even the most orthodox and traditional of monasteries is including social service in its mandate.

Vedanta recognizes the need to go beyond traditions. We may belong to many traditions, but as human beings, we transcend all of them. All traditions are approximations and as such, they will conflict in some aspect. It is the resolution of those conflicts that is the spiritual struggle. And it is that attempt to resolve that leads to innovation. In this struggle, we may be guided by scriptures, but the scriptures are like maps. They will help us, but they will not take us to our destination. This is why the *Gita* and the *Upanishads* speak of the Veda becoming 'aveda': that is, scriptures are no longer necessary. They also say that to the person of illumination, scriptures are like water in a flooded land; they are not necessary.

The *Upanishads* constantly stress the need to question. This is why they speak in aphoristic language and ask the student to contemplate and discover the meaning by themselves. The *Chaandogya Upanishad* says, 'That thou art Svetaketu – find it out.' The *Gita* says that by reverential inquiry, one can learn.

But is this questioning only for certain people? No, it is for all spiritual seekers. The Vivekachudamani of Sankaracharya stresses three conditions for success in spiritual life. The first is a human birth, the second is the desire to be free, and the third is the guidance of a teacher. The desire to be free makes us question.

This questioning should start from where we are and not at some esoteric level. And where we are is our humanity. The best place from which to try to reach God is in understanding our humanity. Swami Sarvagatananda told us the story of a boy from the Arya

Samaj who once came to see Swami Akhandananda. The boy bluntly said, 'I don't believe in God, but I want to be good. What should I do?' Swami Akhandananda told him 'don't hate and don't hurt.' Swami Sarvagatananda observed that these are two very fundamental disciplines for any spiritual aspirant. In the *Gita*, when Sri Krishna is describing the qualities of a devotee of God, the very first quality he states is *advesta*: a devotee does not hate anyone. In the *Yoga Sutras*, when Patanjali is describing the beginning disciplines (*yama*), the first one he mentions is *ahimsa*: one who wishes to be a yogi should not hurt anyone. Thus, Swami Akhandananda's advice 'don't hate, don't hurt' captured two fundamental disciplines as taught by Sri Krishna and by Patanjali.

Sri Sarada Devi (also referred to as the Holy Mother) was asked how we can know whether someone is spiritually awakened or realized. She didn't say anything about sitting in meditation for hours, or about studying the scriptures or performing worship. There are three criteria that the Holy Mother gives us to gauge spiritual evolution, namely that one becomes all-loving, compassionate and deeply concerned about the well-being of others.

Sri Krishna says that a true devotee is one who does not hate anyone, who is friendly and compassionate, who is not very possessive, who does not have an inflated view of himself and who is able to remain balanced in happiness and sadness, and who is forgiving.

Swami Sarvagatananda used to tell us that our behavior is more important than our beliefs, our functioning is more important than our faith and our character is more important than our convictions.

Swami Vivekananda says: "Again, we must consider, religion is a [matter of] growth, not a mass of foolish words. Two thousand years ago a man saw God. Moses saw God in a burning bush. Does what Moses did when he saw God save you? No man's seeing God can help you the least bit except that it may excite you and urge you to do the same thing. That is the whole value of the ancients' examples. Nothing more. [Just] signposts on the way. No man's eating can satisfy another man. No man's seeing God can save another man. You have to see God yourself."[126]

When a plague broke out in Calcutta in 1898, Swami Vivekananda wanted to sell the land that had been recently purchased to house the monastery, and use the money to serve the victims. The proposed monastery would have served as a residence for the monks and as a meeting place for devotees. Swami Vivekananda said that they might as well live under trees which was the ancient tradition for monks, and instead serve human beings in need, which was not the traditional responsibility of monks.

Religion is a matter of spiritual culmination. Swami Vivekananda: "If you [can realise Brahman] by standing on your head, or on one foot, or by worshipping five thousand gods with three heads each – welcome to it! . . . Do it any way you can! Nobody has any right to say anything. Therefore, Krishna says, if your method is better and higher, you have no business to say that another man's method is bad, however wicked you may think it." [127]

In fact, we have to find out for ourselves the disciplines that are effective for us, that will build our character and bring awareness

126 *Complete Works,* Volume 1, p. 469.
127 *Complete Works,* Volume 1, p. 469.

of greater harmony and unity within us. Swami Tyagananda once suggested four such disciplines:

a. Forget all the good things that you have done to others.
b. Forget all the bad things that others have done to you.
c. Be patient.
d. Remember that there is a God.

We will not find these disciplines in any book or scripture, at least not collected together in this way. But they are clearly helpful in spiritual life and they are easy to follow. Failing to customize or individualize spiritual disciplines puts us at risk of entering a 'stupor of the spirit.' We go through the motions of spiritual disciplines but we seem to make no progress.

Consider, for example, the way that we practice meditation. Meditation has three aspects. It begins with concentration. The mind has to become one-pointed. Second, we have to be able to hold the concentration. This is called continuation. Finally, we have to transcend. This is called culmination. When we sit for meditation, are we able to do even the first one? Can we concentrate the mind?

An even more fundamental question is whether we are aware that we are not concentrating the mind. Thoughts are constantly coming and going. Are we getting carried away in those currents, or are we able to hold ourselves apart? Do we know the answer to this question? Many times what happens is that after about ten or fifteen minutes of being carried away by some thought current, we suddenly realize what is happening and remember that we were supposed to be meditating. Sometimes it is even worse. After about half an hour, we suddenly realize that we just had a good nap! It is even worse if we are practicing meditation in a group and we start snoring!

We need to have a good hard look at how we are meditating. What is the quality of that effort? And based on that examination, we should make some intelligent choices. For example, if we feel sleepy at the time set for meditation, then it is better to take a short nap, wash one's face or even take a shower, have a cup of tea or coffee if necessary and enter the shrine room feeling refreshed. If one feels hungry, then have a light snack, and enter the shrine after washing. If the mind is restless, then sing or chant. If you need to sing for one hour before the mind settles down, then sing for one hour. If chanting a few verses is sufficient, then do that.

If the mind is feeling extremely restless, then one can try to memorize something. That effort pulls the mind away from whatever it is brooding on. If your mind feels uninspired, then read something inspiring. Even better, read and take notes. After that, record any thoughts, observations, comments or questions that may come to you while reading. How long should one read? Each person has to judge for themselves.

Reading can be combined with an intermediate kind of contemplation. This may be described as 'meditation on the *lila*.' Take the story of a great soul, for example, the *Gospel of Sri Ramakrishna*. Read a few lines and now try to visualize the scene and the conversation. Try to do this as long as possible. When the mind tries to wander, ask it a question, such as 'what is in that corner of the room?' or 'who else is present in the scene,' and so on. This can be continued for as long as you wish. Not only will it help put the mind in a mood for contemplation. It will also give you the feeling that you spent time with Sri Ramakrishna and that feeling will continue with you even throughout the day.

All of these are examples of simple innovation that we need to work out for ourselves. If we embark on this journey, we shall find that it is the most stimulating adventure we can have. There are many things to discover that are not in books. There is a lot of opportunity to be innovative.

Thinking about the teachings of an innovator such as Swami Vivekananda, and putting them into practice according to our best understanding, can help us see the light of our potential, our innate strengths and our ability to contribute to innovation. *Walk toward that light.* Would that we can all walk toward that light.

Swami Vivekananda says: "religion has just begun. The infinite ocean of spiritual truth lies before us to be worked on, to be discovered, to be brought into our lives. The world has seen thousands of prophets, and the world has yet to see millions . . .

"There were times in olden days when prophets were many in every society. The time is to come when prophets will walk through every street in every city in the world. In olden times, particular, peculiar persons were, so to speak, selected by the operations of the laws of society to become prophets. The time is coming when we shall understand that to become religious means to become a prophet, and that none can become religious until he or she becomes a prophet. We shall come to understand that the secret of religion is not being able to think and say all these thoughts; but, as the Vedas teach, to realize them, *to realise newer and higher ones than have ever been realised, to discover them, bring them to society* [italics added] and the study of religion should be the training to make prophets. The schools and colleges should be training grounds for prophets. The whole universe must become prophets; and until a man becomes a prophet, religion is mockery and a byword unto him. We must see religion, feel it, realise it in a thousand times more intense a sense than that in which we see the wall. . . .

"But there is one principle which underlies all these various manifestations of religion and which has been already mapped out for us. Every science must end where it finds a unity, because we cannot go any further. When a perfect unity is reached, that science has nothing more of principles to tell us. All the work that religions have to do is to work out the details. Take any science, chemistry, for example. Suppose we can find one element out of which we can manufacture all the other elements. Then chemistry, as a science, will have become perfect. What will remain for us is to discover every day new combinations of that one material and the application of those combinations for all the purposes of life. So with religion. The gigantic principles, the scope, the plan of religion were already discovered ages ago when man found the last words, as they are called, of the Vedas—"I am He"—that there is that One in whom this whole universe of matter and mind finds its unity, whom they call God, or Brahman, or Allah, or Jehovah, or any other name. We cannot go beyond that. The grand principle has been already mapped out for us. Our work lies in filling it in, working it out, applying it to every part of our lives. . . .

"We have to work now so that everyone will become a prophet. There is a great work before us. . . ."[128]

This is both an amazing challenge and an amazing invitation. We began with a discussion of how evolution at the human level had moved from the physical to the psycho-social arena. But Swami Vivekananda is asserting that there is a higher level still, and that is to the manifestation of our spiritual nature: a manifestation that does not contradict, but rather fulfills our human destiny. Such a development is the full aim and culmination of the science of human possibilities.

128 *Complete Works*, Volume 6, pp. 9-11.

EPILOGUE

In the more than four decades since that summer day in 1978 when my brother Ram and I excitedly perused the stacks of the MacOdrum Library at Carleton University searching for works on the *Upanishads*, much has changed. Most notably, if that scene were to be re-enacted today, we might be seated leisurely at home, using a search engine running on a laptop to speedily locate the digital versions of the same works.

Through our various devices, we are connected today not only to each other, but also to a dizzying array of knowledge sources. Connectivity, while not yet ubiquitous, has situated us in the position of being able to read the works of the greatest thinkers, listen to the greatest expositors, and to learn from the very best teachers. Undoubtedly, this is a uniquely opportune moment in the history of the world to access the information resources needed to pursue the science of human possibilities.

The volume of content available online is increasing at a staggering rate. According to Statista.com, in 2024 approximately 330 million terabytes of new data were placed online each day. This daily data output is several orders of magnitude larger than the estimated number of sand particles on Earth.

To make sense of this ever-expanding ocean of information, increasingly sophisticated interfaces are being built to curate and personalize this vast storehouse. This curation goes beyond passive general curation — it actively extrapolates from users' past interests and preferences to anticipate their future needs, delivering relevant information even before it is explicitly requested.

And with each passing day, these interfaces are becoming more intelligent. From the crude recommender systems of a few years ago, we now have AI-driven assistants and even human-like robots assisting us not only in knowledge search and knowledge representation, but even in physical tasks.

Our world is on a relentless technological march forward. Every day brings to our attention a new device or application that can accomplish in mere moments what would have previously taken days, weeks, months, or even years of manual effort.

How does all of this impact the science of human possibilities? Some find the pace of change alarming and are concerned that machines will evolve to a position of dominance over humans who will stagnate and become subservient to omniscient machines. And others, in contrast, see in technology's progress as an engine of immense opportunity to accelerate human evolution. I tend to gravitate to the latter view, with one large caveat.

With every step forward in technology, we have been warned that the new approach is going to make older systems irrelevant and obsolete. While this is true in some cases, in others, it has meant that the older systems evolved to embrace the new technology. Television did not make cinema obsolete, but stimulated cinema to provide an even richer experience for movie-goers. More precisely, it stimulated human thought and creativity to evolve cinema to the next stage.

Online courses did not make in-person instruction obsolete. Rather, virtual learning is leading to a richer in-person experience where routine material can be relegated to an asynchronous mode, freeing up in-person class time for more customized and nuanced interaction. In 2001, when MIT introduced OpenCourseWare (OCW) and made all its instructional materials online and freely available, some wondered what the impact would be on applications to MIT for in-person study. Overall, OCW seems to have resulted in more focused and early applications for admission to MIT.

We cannot underestimate the power of the human spirit. I do believe that the technological advances that we are seeing will provide new tools for us to catapult ourselves to more fully discovering and manifesting our potential.

However, there is one large caveat, namely, that this elevation in our potential will be possible only if we take responsibility for our growth. This is the counterpoint to the freedom that we all seek. Freedom and responsibility build upon one another. We cannot assume that our responsibility ends because certain new technologies may have liberated us from tedious tasks and labors.

We are already seeing this in the different ways by which people make use of technology. The television was called an 'idiot box' because of the vacant state of mind of people who spent hours lazily in front of it, not even completely aware of what they were watching and how it was affecting them. But the same television made it possible for us to participate in world-changing and personally inspiring events such as the first human step on the moon.

The science of human possibilities is our choice to champion.

We are seeing many instances of device addiction, with people using the powerful processors on their smartphones to play games. On the other hand, villagers in various parts of the world are using their smartphones to more effectively time their fishing or planting, or to be instantly paid for their services. The same phone can also inform us of things that will help us to grow, to leverage our true talents, and to make progress towards our goals.

It is our choice to immerse ourselves in the science of human possibilities.

And thus it will be with artificial intelligence. We need to build the frameworks that will make AI an enabler of human growth and an engine for the science of human possibilities to harness. I am optimistic that we will seize this opportunity.

The science of human possibilities is our choice to cultivate individually, and together.

PLACE AND NAME INDEX